OVER
–AND–
OUT

JAMES F JORDAN

ISBN: 1482048019
ISBN-13: 9781482048018
Library of Congress Control Number: 2013901409
CreateSpace Independent Publishing Platform
North Charleston, South Carolina

INTRODUCTION

It was February 1968. Everyone in my neighborhood was talking about Vietnam, and a lot of guys were joining the different branches of the military services; it was all over the news and TV. It was nonstop reporting about Vietnam and that the United States must do something to stop communism. I decided to enlist in the United States Marine Corps. I knew the Marine Corps was for me because my older brother, Jack, was a marine. I dropped out of high school and went to the recruiting office with my friend Butch, and we each enlisted for a two-year active duty tour. My recruiter told me that because I was only seventeen, I would need my parents' permission to enlist, and they had to cosign my enlistment papers.

I took my papers home and waited for my parents to arrive home from work. I told them that my wish was to be a marine, just like my brother. We were an Irish Catholic family who was big on tradition, and my father had served as a staff sergeant in the army during World War II. I figured I could do no less than he and Jack had.

My father told me he was very proud of me, but my mother was a hard sell. My mom knew all too well what war was like, having lost a cousin at Pearl Harbor and a brother wounded in Italy, and my father had gone through hell with a tank division in North Africa. My mom kept saying that she knew all about the suffering and cost of war. She didn't want me to join at all. But after getting them to cosign my papers, I went back to the recruiting office the very next day, and Butch and I signed up for two years of active duty. We went to downtown Philadelphia, and with a big group of guys, we all took our oath together.

Nineteen sixty-eight was a leap year. We left Philadelphia on February 29, bound for Parris Island, South Carolina. We drove onto the island by bus late in the day, and that was the beginning of a very long and hard basic training. We had four drill instructors, and they each had their own personalities, but they were all Marine Corps all day and all night. The top sergeant was Gunnery Sergeant Winn, and he was big and mean and put fear in me. I was afraid to mess up on anything I did because he would get right in my face if I fouled up. All of us were afraid of all four of them, but especially the gunny.

From sunup to sundown, all we did was exercise and drill. There were about fifty guys in our platoon, and we were from all walks of life. Throughout basic training I learned a lot about myself and other people. I was pushed to the point that I thought I could not do any more and then found another level inside myself that gave me the strength to do better at everything I did. I think we all felt the same way.

Butch and I were right next to each other all the time because we were always placed in alphabetical order. My name started with a J and his with a K. So we talked every chance we could. After about five weeks, the drill sergeants told us while we were at formation that a couple of guys were being sent back a class because they were not where they should be, and Butch was one of them. I remember how sad it was for both of us when he left that day.

I graduated from boot camp in May 1968 and went home on leave. I couldn't wait to get home after eight weeks of basic training. My mom and dad and my three brothers greeted me with open arms, and they were very proud of me. I could feel it the whole time I was home. My father asked me everything he could about everything I saw and did, and my brother, Jack, who was in the Marine Corps Reserve at that time, knew exactly what I had been through. But my mom couldn't give a hoot about me becoming a marine. All she worried about was where was I going and when I was going. I could see the fear and worry in her eyes and in her voice, and it seemed like I couldn't do or say anything to change that. She went to mass twice a day, and she liked it when I went with her. I often thought that I hurt her in some way because day after day all the news talked about was Vietnam, on the radio and TV and in the newspapers, and all of our neighbors told my mom that I would probably be sent there, and that made her more upset.

After thirty days of leave, I reported for training in jungle warfare in North Carolina for a few more weeks. In basic training I had become skilled with an M14 rifle, but when we got to jungle warfare, we were given M16 rifles, and we had to learn how to clean and operate them. Jungle warfare was a whole different kind of training. We were now training in very thick weeds and lots of trees. It was very hot, and we learned everything we could about booby traps and hand signals.

We were on patrol one day, and the guy next to me was from the south, and he kept telling me how much he loved the woods and creeks and it was like home to him. I told him he was nuts. He tapped me on the shoulder, and when I turned around, he was holding a big, nasty-looking snake and started licking his lips. I again told him that he was definitely nuts, and that made him smile even more. Then one of the instructors told him to walk away and let the snake go. He was pissed off and mumbled as he walked away.

We learned all we could about smoke grenades. They even put us in a room and threw in gas grenades. What an experience that was. I then graduated that school, and we all waited around for our orders. This was the time we had all been waiting for. We had completed our training and schooling. This was the time when we would be told what MOS (military occupational specialty) we would have and where each of us would be sent. We all just sat around talking about where we were going and wondering what our job titles would be. I wanted to be in the infantry, but some guys didn't. Everyone was nervous.

Sure enough, a sergeant came walking out of a building and posted our names on a big billboard. The orders were real easy to read because all of our names were in alphabetical order. Those orders told us what our MOSes were and where we were going. We all crowded around that billboard, trying to find our names. When I got close enough, I saw my name, and my MOS was 0311, which was infantry, and my destination was Vietnam. I felt relieved, and I heard guys cursing and saw guys high-fiving and yelling. But as it sunk in where I was going, I could only think of my mom, and I knew that I had to tell her. Then everybody was asking everyone else where they were going and what their MOSes were. Most of us were going to Vietnam; some of the guys went on embassy duty, and some of the guys went to Europe and Japan.

At that time they sent us home on leave. I don't know why I was in such a hurry to go to Vietnam, but I was. I went back home and told my parents that they were sending me to Vietnam. It didn't bother me at all, but my father and mother were devastated. I felt like I had picked up a bat and hit my mom and dad with it. My brothers and my uncle were jumping up and down. As I shook their hands, I looked at my parents hugging each other and not letting go. At that point my emotions were split in half.

After a while things calmed down. Mom went to church, and my father sat down with a cup of coffee and told me that he had stood in my shoes before and knew where I was going and what to expect. He then shook my hand and hugged me and told me not to worry about Mom's reaction. He told me moms were just like that. I kept assuring them that I would be OK and come home as soon as my tour of duty was up. And I told my mother that they needed guys like me to help the United States stop communism. I really believed that.

My parents did everything they could to make me feel wanted and needed in the thirty days that I was home. I never forgot that. My leave was up, and it was time to go, so I went to the Philadelphia airport and boarded my flight to San Diego. I had a coach seat, but they put me in first class. I had never flown first class before, and I sat there all alone. I looked out the window, knowing my family was waiting for my flight to take off, and in a way I was glad for my parents that I was finally leaving.

The jet took off, and as we flew away, I knew I was on my way to the other side of the world. During my flight the attendants treated me like a king and made me feel special. I went to the restroom and noticed there weren't many people onboard.

I arrived in California, proceeded to Camp Pendleton, and reported in. We stayed there about two weeks, and then we all got shipping orders. I was heading for Okinawa. Once in Okinawa we were assigned to different camps, and we were one step closer to our final destination. I stayed in a camp about three days, and then I got my orders for an airplane flight to Vietnam. At that time I was told I was to be part of the First Marine Division, but I still didn't know where I was going.

As we waited to board our flight, all kinds of uniforms were getting on that jet—air force, army, marines. There were no empty seats. For the most part, the flight was quiet. The crew was really nice to us, and it wasn't long before we were told to buckle up because we were approaching Danang. We had heard rumors that some of the planes had been shot at while landing in Vietnam. I couldn't help looking at the floor as we descended, hoping not to see any bullets. We were all kind of nervous. I stared at the floor the whole time until we landed.

We all got off the plane, and it seemed like everybody was in a hurry. We heard a Marine Corps sergeant with a bullhorn telling all marines to stand next to him and await further orders. I didn't know where I was going, but that sergeant had our names, and he called them out one by one and told us what group to get in. I knew I was with the First Division, but I waited to find out exactly what outfit I would be placed with.

About ten of us were told to form a group, and once we did that, he said he would get right back to us. We watched the sergeant run from one group to the next, dispatching every group in an orderly fashion. Then he came right back to us and told us to board a certain helicopter. We were going to a base called Phu Bai. The ten of us were going to the Second Battalion, First Marine (2/1) Division.

He yelled, "Good luck, men," and we took off.

As we took off, we stared out of the back of the chopper, looking at all of the movement on the ground and all the choppers flying around. The ten of us, five on one side and five on the other, just looked at each other, holding our gear. We couldn't hear anything but the blades of the chopper.

Within an hour we landed in Phu Bai, and there was a truck waiting for us. We got on and were driven to a camp that looked empty. We were told that the Second Battalion, First Marines had been relocated; we'd just missed them. We were told to stay in one of the hooches and await orders. They put the ten of us on guard duty for the night and spread us out in foxholes, two guys in each hole. They told us they would check on us throughout the night.

We watched as the sun went down. I suddenly realized where I was, what I was doing, and how hot it was. My partner and I were both quiet and nervous all night long. No talking was allowed, and my eyes went back and forth hour after hour. It was a very long night. We were surprised by the heat all night. All was quiet that night.

When the sun started to rise, we were told to go back to the hooch and get some sleep. We went by helicopter to catch up with the Second Battalion, First Marines. We were flown to where a truck waited to take us to the 2/1 compound. The ten of us were now on our way to our final destination. It was about a forty-five-minute ride to the compound.

We looked out at the countryside as we rode along. It was all new to us. None of us said a word. We just kept looking at the people, some on bikes, some on scooters, some just walking, some carrying stuff, some not. The road was very busy with both military and civilian people; everyone seemed to be going somewhere all at once. We could see the compound off in the distance. It seemed like a mound of sand from where we were, but as we got closer we could see the tops of the hooches.

Once inside we were taken to the 2/1 headquarters. The ten of us got out of the truck, and a sergeant with a clipboard took a roll call. He officially welcomed us to 2/1. He explained to us that the battalion consisted of Echo Company, Foxtrot Company, Golf Company, Hotel Company, and H&S and scouts recon. He told us what companies we were to report to. He took us around the compound, explaining how each company had their own sector. When we got to Golf Company, he called my name and another guy's name. He told us this would be our new home, and we were handed over to a sergeant from Golf Company. He shook our hands and welcomed us. The sergeant gave us a tour of the camp. He showed us the mess hall, the latrines, and an official sign saying, "Welcome to Golf Company, Platoons 1/2/3."

We were taken to the Second Platoon and placed in Bravo Squad. I didn't know it at the time, but it would be my home for my whole tour of duty. Our sergeant introduced us to our squad leader and then walked away. I thought to myself, *I'm finally here. So this is what it's like. Sure is hot.* Our squad leader introduced himself to us as George. I wasn't sure of his last name, but I think it was Prescott. He took us to a hooch and said, "This is Bravo Squad's hotel; come on in and pick a suite."

He asked our names and where we were from. I told him I was Jim Jordan from Philadelphia. The guy next to me said he was also from Philadelphia and his name was Harrison. We looked at one another, and the squad leader started to laugh. "It's a small world," he said. "What's the odds that both of you today are from Philadelphia?"

He told us to go in and store our stuff, and he would introduce us to the squad and get our gear. We met the guys and got our gear, and George told us to go outside. He told us Bravo Squad had just taken a beating. "We could use more guys, but two guys are OK by me." He told me that I would be his new radioman and that Harrison would become his point man. He explained that the frame of my body was more suited for a radio than Harrison's. Whatever the reason, I was now a radioman for Bravo Squad.

George said he would give me a crash course on the radio and that Harrison would learn to be a point man. He explained to us what was expected of us. "Patrols are what we do; ambushes at night, patrols in the daytime. If we go out at night, we sleep in the daytime. If we go out in the day, we sleep at night." He told us that we would rotate a lot. We would guard and patrol a bridge and sometimes guard the POW camp. All those guys in the squad were very nice to us. They treated us like brothers; they didn't treat us like rookies, and we liked that.

I didn't sleep much that first night. I could hear artillery fire all night long; it didn't seem to bother anybody else. I got up early that morning, about 6:50 a.m. We were told that we would be going out on patrol at eight o'clock. I tried to do what the other guys did. We washed up, went to the bathroom, and headed for the mess hall. I was quite surprised by how good the food was. They had cold cereal, fresh fruit, eggs, and potatoes. Breakfast was my favorite meal of the day, anyhow, so I enjoyed the heck out of it.

After eating we went back to our hooch. I watched what the other guys were doing. They cleaned their rifles and checked their gear and waited for roll call. Roll call was very fast because squads were out on patrol and some squads were asleep, so there weren't many heads to count. Roll call ended close to eight o'clock, so we all went back to the hooch to suit up. I had never used or operated a radio before, so this was all new to me.

MY FIRST PATROL

I put my radio on and checked my gear. I followed the guys to the exit area for our company. Once we got to the rim of the sand dune, we lined up. At that time George told Harrison he would be third in line going out. The point man was first, followed by the cover man, and then Harrison and George. I was to be the fifth man in back, followed by the rest of the squad. There were nine of us that day. George told me to call Golf Company and tell them Golf Two Bravo was ready for departure, over and out. Golf Company said, "Roger, over and out."

George told us all to lock and load. He then told the point man which direction to head in. One by one, about six to eight feet apart, we departed from the compound. There was a bunker right next to the pathway that led in and out. It was always manned by guards. As we walked by the bunker one by one, the guards called out encouragement and good luck. It was the first time I walked through that pathway. As I looked down, I could see all the claymore mines and barbed wire everywhere. We kept zigzagging through the wire. It took us quite a few minutes to walk through that corridor. Finally we were through and on our way to a tree line, slow and easy.

I was looking ahead at the point man. He had a long and thin light stick, and he tapped it on the ground in a rhythmic manner. He used that stick to penetrate the ground in front of him. When we got to the tree line, he lifted it in the air to feel for any wires. It took real talent. As the point man was doing that, the cover man behind him would look over the point man's shoulder and to his left and right, always watching for movement of any kind. He protected the point man at all times; that was his job. Harrison watched the point man and every move he made.

I was about to step into my first rice paddy. I learned fast to stay off the trails because they were heavily booby-trapped, so we went from one rice paddy to the next on our way to checkpoint one. Some of the rice paddies were deep, up your belly button, and some were shallow, up to your knees; you never knew from one to the next.

Finally, after about two hours, we reached checkpoint one. George told me to call Golf Company and tell them that Golf Two Bravo had reached checkpoint one. Golf Company acknowledged and said, "Over and out." George knelt down, getting his map and compass out, and mapped our next course to checkpoint two. He told the point man which direction to go and then told me to call Golf Company and radio in, "Golf Two Bravo departing for check-point two, over and out."

We then headed in a different direction, being very quiet all the way. There were many stops along the way. Sometimes the cov-er man would think he'd seen or heard something and would raise his hand. We would all drop to one knee. We would stop, look, and listen. Sometimes it was an animal. We were very cautious at all times. Anytime someone raised his hand, I thought something was about to happen, and I kept my eyes on the squad leader, awaiting orders. I was ready. I was nervous and scared as I slowly turned around to see what the other guys were doing. I could see their helmets turning left and right. I could hear the sound of choppers off in the distance and thought, *So this is Vietnam.* I had the feeling that we all felt the tension in that underbrush. After a few moments, we were on our way again.

We reached checkpoint two, and I called Golf Company and told them Golf Two Bravo had reached checkpoint two. Our squad leader got down on one knee, got out his compass and map, and mapped our course to checkpoint three. While he was doing that, I was nervous. I didn't know what contact was going to be like, and I knew that the whole squad would count on me to use our radio in the heat of the battle, so I kept telling myself to be ready when they needed me. George would tell the point man which direction to go, and then he would tell me to radio Golf Company and tell them we were proceeding to checkpoint three. That was basically how a patrol was run.

The heat was unbearable to me. My radio started to get heavy at this point. I started to realize where I was, what I was doing, and who I was with. We went through rice paddy after rice paddy, and I had the soggiest socks in the world. I couldn't help but realize just how professional these guys were. I was learning from the best, and I knew it.

We reached checkpoint three, and there was still no contact with the enemy. Our squad leader got down on his knee, got his map and compass out, and mapped a course back to the compound. I radioed Golf Company and told them we had reached checkpoint three with no contact, and were heading back to base. It was so hot, and we were all sweating like crazy, especially Harrison and me because we were not used to such extreme heat. The sun felt so powerful. I had never seen so many rice paddies.

We started heading back to base, slow and easy, always looking, always listening. Everybody had everybody's backs; it was just that simple. My first patrol that day lasted about eight hours. We were getting close to base, so we stopped, and I radioed back to Golf that we were nearing the edge of the tree line of the compound. That's when Golf Company alerted the guards in the bunkers that we were returning. We came out at the tree line and headed back to the path that would take us through the barbed wire corridor, zigzagging back into the compound. As we walked one by one past the bunker, the guys inside would say, "Welcome back, nice job," and sometimes nothing was said.

Once we were inside, George told us to unload and clear our weapons. I couldn't wait to get the radio off my back. I followed the guys back to the hooch and watched while some of them went right to sleep and others wrote letters home. Harrison and I just looked at one another with sighs of relief, both of us glad that our first patrol was over.

MY SECOND PATROL

The next day our squad leader told us that our next patrol would be a night ambush. We would leave the compound about one hour before dusk. That day all the guys did was clean their weapons and sleep. Everyone seemed to be real close. I could tell they were all like brothers. I was fortunate to have three brothers in my family, and these guys were close. I wrote a couple letters home, telling my parents and friends that I had arrived safely. I told them my new mailing address, that I was a radioman in a squad with seasoned veterans, and that I was in good company. I reassured my mother.

After waiting around all day, we went for an early dinner again. I was surprised again by how good the food was. The cooks treated us like kings. They told us we could eat as much as we could and that they would cook us eggs anytime we wanted them. The cooks kept coming over to our table, asking if we wanted more after dinner.

We headed back to the hooch to get ready for our departure. Guys were constantly checking their weapons and ammo. A couple guys reminded me to go to the bathroom before we left because it would be a long night. They told me I would not be able to take a shit out there so to go now. Those guys knew exactly when to get up and get ready, so I did what they did, got ready when they did, and then we slowly made our way to the departure point. Everybody positioned themselves in line. I saw our squad leader heading toward us with a map and compass.

A night ambush was different than a regular patrol. For the night ambush, we would travel to a designated spot, position ourselves, and wait for any enemy movement. When we were ready to depart the compound, we'd head for a designated spot determined by Golf Company. We were told to lock and load, and we started to leave one by one, saying good-bye to the guys in the bunker. We were all in the same positions as the day before as we zigzagged through the wire. I radioed in to Golf Company: "Exiting the compound, over and out." They responded and we were on our way.

It was August. I was surprised by how hot it was at that time of day. We could see the sun starting to go down. The squad leader kept the compass in his hand at all times, looking at his map constantly. It was starting to get pretty dark. We were going through rice paddy after rice paddy. My radio got heavier and heavier and started to feel like a ton of bricks on my back. Someone up front heard something, so we stopped. The water was up to my chest.

I hadn't been trained on how to operate a radio, but I realized that my squad was counting on me to call for help if we needed it. I tried to keep the radio dry, so I stood on my toes as high as I could. The bugs were biting me like crazy, and I was sweating a lot. I couldn't do anything but stand there and take it. This was a lot worse than my first patrol. I felt like the bugs were attacking me on purpose. It took every ounce of my self-control not to swat just one single bug. The sweat was pouring out of me.

That night was the worst night of my life. My back was killing me, and the bugs were all over my face and neck, just chomping away. I had my rifle over my head, and we just stood there. It seemed like forever. I kept looking at the other guys, wondering if they were nervous, but everyone was quiet, and nobody moved an inch. I thought my back was going to break, but finally we started to move again.

It was almost pitch-black, but we were close to our ambush site, so I was afraid to complain. Once we arrived, our squad leader positioned all of us, and we put out our claymore mines, sat down, and got comfortable. Claymore mines were small explosives that you stuck in the ground facing away from you. They gave you strong support if you were attacked. It started to rain that night, and boy did it rain. It felt funny just sitting there in the teeming rain, but that's what we did.

As soon as the rain stopped, the mosquitoes started up again. It sounded like a million of them were under my helmet. I couldn't talk. I couldn't slap at them; all I could do was rub bug spray on my skin. That night I used a whole bottle of it, but it didn't help. When it started to rain again, the bugs would stop. It was the only relief I got. I had been in rainstorms before, but not like this. It was like turning a garden hose on full throttle. I was wondering how the hell anybody could live in a place like this. I wished it never stopped raining that night, but it was off and on all night long. At least the radio was off my back.

It was so dark that night and so quiet. I was sitting next to my squad leader all night and kept looking at the other guys, just sitting, looking in all directions, holding their weapons. I was waiting all night for something to happen. We had no visitors that night. As the sun was starting to rise, we all got up, stretched out, and tried to clear the water off our weapons the best we could, but we had nothing dry to do it with.

I radioed back to Golf that we were heading back to base. We headed back, stopping about five hundred yards away, and I called in and told them that we were almost at the tree line, over and out, again. Golf Company notified the guards that we were coming in, and we headed right for the path, zigzagging our way back into the compound.

Inside, our squad leader told us to unload and clear our weapons and dry out. That's exactly what we did, and then we ate breakfast. I think I was the first in line, and I was hungry, extra portions for me please, and they piled it on. As we sat at the table, I mentioned how hellish that night was for me, but the guys just kind of laughed and said I would get used to it, and I went back for more food.

MY THIRD PATROL

S cheduled for a daytime patrol, we had formation at eight o'clock, and then after roll call we were dismissed. We were told to eat because our patrol would take off at ten o'clock. We went out through the wire. Harrison was still learning how to be a point man, and I was still learning how to be a radio man. It was hot and sunny, and our squad leader told the point man which way to go. As we walked I turned around to see what the other guys were doing. They would smile and give the thumbs up, but they never took their eyes off our surroundings.

We were about one hour out when a very big blast happened at the front of our patrol. It was big and loud; everybody hit the ground. The silence after the blast seemed just as loud. The cover man yelled back that the point man was gone. We all stood up one by one, looking up at a cloud of smoke just floating up and away. I didn't know what had happened. I stood there not knowing what to do.

My squad leader told me to contact Golf Company and tell them we had just encountered a bomb or a mine and were missing our point man. Golf Company told us to spread out and search for the point man. We could not find anything. No body, no blood, no weapon—nothing. I kept thinking that there had to be something, but no one found anything. Then somebody yelled that he had found an empty boot. That was all that was left: a boot with nothing in it.

I saw it and didn't know what to think. Our squad leader told me to call Golf Company to report that our point man was killed in action. Golf Company told us to continue on our patrol, and we did. I remember stopping and looking everywhere for any remains, but there was nothing. As we walked away, I could not believe what had happened. I forget the guy's name, but I remember he had blond hair and wore an old French flak jacket and a feather in his helmet. I could see that everyone was angry, and I felt the mournfulness all around me.

As we kept walking, I realized that was Harrison's and my first encounter with the Vietcong (VC). We couldn't see the VC, but I could feel them all around us. Harrison was now our point man; he learned fast.

After about five hours, we finished our patrol. Everybody looked pissed off on our way back to the compound. The guys later told me that it was probably a bomb dropped by a plane or a jet that had never gone off and had been rigged as a booby trap by the VC.

Harrison and I learned that day, and as time went by, that all we did was patrol, patrol, ambush, and patrol. I liked being a radio operator. I was getting really good with the lingo needed to use it properly, and Harrison was getting lots of experience at point.

MY FIRST FIREFIGHT

That night we were told that we would be going out on another daytime patrol. We left the compound and were out for about two hours. All of a sudden, a hail of bullets was flying all around us. Everyone hit the ground and started to fire back. It was the first time in my life that I heard the sound of an AK-47 rifle. I could not see anybody, and the bullets were still flying over our heads.

I lay on the ground, scared, and tried in vain to fire my rifle. At that moment I realized this was what I had been trained for, but I did not realize that my radio was right behind my helmet, so every time I tried to lift my head to fire my rifle, my radio would stop my head from moving up. I kept thinking that if I kept lying there on my stomach the VC would walk up and put a bayonet in me. So I rolled to my side and tried to see if my squad leader was OK. Then I yelled, asking if he wanted me to call Golf.

All the time those AK-47 rounds were going right over my head. I never fired a round that day, but I almost broke my neck trying to. George told me to stand by. Then he put his arm up, and the shooting suddenly stopped. All was quiet and no one was hurt. George looked at me, staring at my helmet, and then he started smiling because there was sand falling out of it. At that point I felt embarrassed because he might have seen me lying there, trying in vain to shoot back. I explained to him what had happened to me, and he put his hand on my shoulder and said, "Next time fall down on your side or take a knee." Then he took off my helmet, banged the sand out, and put it back on my head. Then he checked to make sure we were all OK.

He told us to get ready to move out. As we started out, he said to me, "That was a normal firefight." He said that a lot of times the VC wanted you to chase them and run into booby traps that they had waiting. I looked at Harrison, and he looked back at me, and we nodded at each other. After we finished our patrol, when we got back to camp, we went to our hooch. George told me he was getting close to going home. He handed me a .45 pistol in a holster and told me to wear it at all times and use it when I couldn't use my rifle. I liked George. Then he said we were all brothers and asked me to watch his back. It was at that moment I knew I was family.

It seemed like Golf Company kept rotating our platoons. One platoon would be on patrol while another platoon was protecting the bridge that was nearby, a third was guarding the nearby POW camp, and guard duty at the compound constantly rotated every couple weeks.

We were standing at our morning formation when our captain told us that a K-9 German shepherd dog and his handler were joining us. They would be going out with us for a couple of days. It was a test to see if this dog could find and pinpoint any trip wires or freshly dug mines. We thought the idea was great and were eager to find out what this dog could do, so we fell out of formation talking about the dog, but we were looking forward to the test.

It was sunny and hot again. We left the compound, zigzagging our way out through the wire. It was a very simple patrol, straight to one location and right back in basically the same way. We were all watching the dog and his handler. I don't remember his name; he was a sergeant and seemed like a nice guy. They stayed right behind the cover man. We kept going, waiting for the handler to say OK, that they would take over point, but he never did. All he did was talk to that dog and give him treats. We finished the three-hour patrol, and the dog never walked point.

When we got back to the base, our squad leader told our lieutenant what had happened. The lieutenant asked the handler how it went, and he said the dog was just not ready to take point, so we would go out the next day and try it all over again. I don't know where the dog and his handler slept that night, but it wasn't in our hooch with us.

Next morning, at eight o'clock formation, the dog and his handler were there, and we were told that at noontime that our patrol would leave. Some guys went back to bed, some guys ate breakfast, and some wrote home or read their mail.

Noontime came and we were all ready for patrol. We zigzagged through the wire and headed in a different direction; again it was just a simple patrol, straight out and straight back. Again the handler with the dog next to him was right behind the cover man. We kept wondering why this dog was not doing what he was supposed to. Finally our squad leader told us to stop halfway through our patrol. He told the handler that the dog would never learn if it wasn't given a chance. The handler got mad and said the dog was just not ready. He said he would tell us when his dog was ready and not when we said he was ready, period. The handler was upset, but so were we.

I knew my squad leader was pissed off. I could hear George cursing in a low voice. We all felt the same way. When we took a break, we all agreed that we were walking all over for nothing and we all knew that handler loved his dog and was overprotective, and he would not put that said dog on point, period.

We headed back to the base again. As soon as we were all inside, our squad leader told us to unload. I saw him head right for headquarters. All night long we talked about the dog. Harrison and I both liked dogs, but we both felt like we were risking our lives by taking that dog for a walk. We just couldn't figure out why this dog was not doing what he had been brought here to do. We sat up all night talking about that dog. We all knew that the handler was the problem, but George spoke up and said, "Orders are orders, guys."

It was day three, and once again we were given an easy patrol, out and back. This time our squad leader stopped the patrol after about fifteen minutes. He told the dog handler, "It's time now." The squad leader told him that this was the last day for the dog to learn. We could all feel the tension in the air.

The handler took the leash off the dog, and they went to the point. The squad leader told them which way to go. We started, and it was so slow that we were crawling along. I kept looking at our squad leader; I could see how mad he was. George kept wiping the sweat off his forehead and looking at his watch. The handler told the dog to go in a certain direction, and then after about three feet he would call the dog back. He would give the dog a treat and kept petting him, telling him how good he was. That went on for thirty minutes, and then they stopped.

We knew then that the handler was in love with that dog. We just watched for thirty minutes as the handler sweated like crazy and hugged that dog. We knew; we all knew. We were all looking at that handler, but he would not look at us. The handler said that was enough, and he put the leash back on and petted that dog over and over and over again, treat after treat.

We went back to the base, and once inside the handler stood and told us thanks for taking them along and good luck to all of us. We never saw them again. (*Good riddance.*)

RAT PATROL

mmmf FResh WATeR!

After two weeks of patrolling and ambushes, our platoon was sent to a bridge called Two Cal to relieve another platoon for the next two weeks. Guarding the bridge was a nice job. We mostly sat around, checked people's IDs, and inspected whatever they were carrying. Alpha, Bravo, and Charlie squads were there, and a Sergeant Peeler was in charge. All day long we just watched the civilians walk back and forth over that bridge, mostly women and senior citizens and lots of kids. If anyone was older than sixteen or seventeen, we checked them out thoroughly, but there weren't many of them.

We took turns going out on ambushes at night, which meant Bravo Squad went out every third night. We liked that a lot. Every sunup we would see the mine sweepers on foot, walking right up to the bridge. They came from the 2/1 compound, which was not that far away. That road had to be checked for mines every day. At night the VC would dig mines in the road and then run away.

After they declared that the road was safe, all kinds of trucks, tanks, and jeeps would travel on it all day long. There was a rat patrol that drove up and down the road all day long. A rat patrol is a jeep with four guys in it: the driver, a shotgun, and two guys in the back with M60 machine guns. That's all they did was ride that road, and at nighttime they would go very slow. I remember thinking, *I hope I never have to ride with them.* It seemed like it was not a very good job. I think at nighttime they only traveled once or twice a night, very slowly and very quietly.

We were at Two Cal Bridge, and it was our turn to go on night ambush, which was no big deal because ambushes were only about one or two hours. Out we walked in one big circle, and when we were almost to our ambush site, we stopped at Two Cal Road. It was getting dark, and our course took us over that road. Our squad leader told us to cross the road one by one until we were all over it. Harrison went first, and then we heard the rat patrol coming. We didn't know what to do. I could see our squad leader, and he was scared, so I was getting nervous. The rat patrol didn't know we were there, and we weren't expecting them. Something had to give.

We could hear the engine of the jeep coming closer and closer. We knew they would open fire on us if they heard anything or saw any movement. Maybe they had seen Harrison cross the road; maybe they had seen one of us move because there was a tiny bit of light left.

The rat patrol slowly stopped. Those seemed like the longest seconds in my life, and my heart was pounding like crazy. Then our squad leader started singing the Marine Corps anthem out loud, and we all started to sing together, louder and louder. That's when the rat patrol started shooting their M60s in our direction. We were all singing the Marine Corps anthem as loudly as we could. Bullets and tracers were flying over our heads and all around us, but we kept singing, "From the halls of Montezuma…"

I kept my head down behind a little clump of concrete from an old blown-up pagoda, thinking, *Hey, guys—it's us.* I turned my head sideways, trying to sing in their direction. The shooting stopped, and we kept singing as loudly as we could—they had heard us. There was silence everywhere, but we kept singing.

The jeep pulled up, and they started yelling at us, and we yelled right back at them. We explained that we were on patrol and on course. No one had told them that we were supposed to be in the area. I called back to headquarters and told them we had encountered the rat patrol, that they fired over our heads but there were no casualties. I was really shaken up that night, and so were those guys in the jeep. Ever since that night, when I hear that Marine Corps anthem, I think of where I was and who I was with and how loudly I once sang that anthem.

After about two weeks at the bridge, we went back to the base, back on patrols again. Booby traps all the time. It seemed like at night the VC would plant all kinds of trip wire, mostly on trails, which was why we never used the trails, because they had so many booby traps. But Harrison would find them, no matter where they were. We would call headquarters to tell them we found booby traps and where we found them and then destroy them. We were very good at that. Search and destroy, search and destroy. And that's exactly what we did. We must have made a lot of VC mad because we ruined their little surprises.

We would then head back to base, and once inside the compound we would unlock and unload and go back to our hooch. When the sun went down, there were no loud noises and no lights. Sometimes at night the VC would shoot a couple of rockets into our base just to let us know they were out there. After a while it seemed like the rockets didn't bother anybody; it was like, "OK, I'm all right; good night."

We were told the next morning that we were going on an operation so we should check our gear and get ready. I didn't know what an operation was like, but I was about to find out. An operation involved the whole battalion. All of us would be airlifted by helicopter to a designated spot and then disembark and wait.

It took a lot of helicopters to transport all of us, but we all landed at the same time. Each company—Echo, Foxtrot, Hotel, and Golf—lined up with each other, one big line of companies next to each other. Each company had three platoons, and each platoon had three squads. We also had an M60 squad and a mortar squad; that was a lot of firepower. We would all get in position, kneel down, and await orders.

Our captain would walk from platoon to platoon, telling everyone to get ready to move out and sweep and clear. There was a lot of talk on my radio, and I just listened to it. All I could hear was 2/1 headquarters telling each platoon leader to start out in ten minutes. So there we went.

It was a normal hot, sunny day, and we started out slowly, making sure everyone was in line. Our captain kept asking me if we were between Alpha and Charlie squads, and I would reply, "Affirmative, over and out." There was a reason we had been put at that location, and it was because it was occupied by a lot of VC. As we pressed forward, we would flush out a lot of VC in hiding and chase them down. Choppers were flying right over our heads with their machine gunners blasting away at the VC running away, but not all the VC ran, so we had to find them one by one. That was the difficult part. They were dug in real good and very hard to spot. We were all yelling at each other: "be careful," "watch where you're walking," "look for wires," "stay on line," "look for holes," and "slow and easy."

All along our line, you could hear gunfire on both sides of us. Our platoon leader was telling us not to get ahead of the companies next to us. We just kept moving forward. The radio was going crazy. It was hard to understand who was who on the radio. Then all of a sudden battalion headquarters told everyone to stay off the radio because there was just too much activity going on at once. So headquarters told us to report in company by company, and that's what we did. Our platoon leader would check up on his three squads and report back to the company commander. It was like a machine that kept moving forward.

When one of us was wounded, we had helicopter medevacs there in two minutes or less. A lot of guys were wounded that day, but we wiped out a very large number of VC and NVA (North Vietnamese Army) soldiers and captured a lot of arms and ammo. We pissed Charlie off that day and every day after. Sweep and clear—and that's what we did. It lasted for days, and now I knew what an operation was like.

ROAD DUTY

After the operation Bravo Squad was sent to a checkpoint on the road that went from 2/1 Battalion to a small village nearby. Our squad leader completed his tour of duty and started his trip home, so we now had a new leader. His name was Roger Moore. Roger was a member of Bravo Squad. There was a small bunker at the village, and we checked IDs and inspected whatever the civilians were carrying. A jeep pulled up to us, and we got a new replacement for our squad. We introduced ourselves and welcomed him with open arms. We explained to him what we were doing and that we would stay at that checkpoint until dusk and then hike back to the compound. The next morning after breakfast, we would hike back to that checkpoint and start all over again.

On that second day, I asked our newest member where he was from. He told me he was from Texas and that he was a cook at a very nice restaurant. He pointed to a large flock of ducks that were sitting in water and said, "See those ducks over there?" I said yes. He said if I got him one of those ducks, he would cook and serve us the best cooked dinner we ever had. So I looked at the ducks just sitting in about six inches of water, and I got up and started walking toward the ducks. I yelled back at him to start a fire. I pulled out my. 45 pistol and headed for a big white duck and started shooting for its neck. It was hard to do because my .45 was not very accurate, but after about six shots, I got it.

I picked the duck up and carried it back. I said, "Let's see how good of a cook you are." He took the duck and told me to have a seat in the lounge and that we would be called when dinner was ready.

About five minutes later, a captain came walking up to us and asked who shot the duck. I said, "I did, sir." He asked me my name and told me to follow him. I went with him and we headed right for the village. When I got to the middle of the village, I saw a tent, and inside were a couple of officers, an elderly villager sitting on the ground, and a marine colonel with a translator talking to him. It seemed that these officers had been going to 2/1 headquarters when they were flagged down by the villagers screaming that some-one had shot their duck. As we approached the tent, the captain told me that the colonel wanted to see me right now. I could see that everybody looked pissed off, and I knew it was curtains for me.

I stood in front of the colonel and saluted him. He asked me my name, rank, serial number, and what outfit I was with, and I told him. He asked me if I had shot a duck, and I said, "Yes, sir, I did." He then asked me why, and I told him why. The old guy sit-ting on the ground told the translator that I was the guy who had shot his favorite duck and that he was heartbroken. The colonel asked the translator to ask the guy what it would take to remedy the situation, and the old guy said thirty dollars and an apology. The colonel told me to pay him thirty dollars, but I told the colo-nel that I had no money. The colonel told me that he would pay the thirty dollars and it would be taken out of my next paycheck, which it was. He then told me to apologize to the guy and give him the dead duck, which I did. They folded up the tent, and that fast they were gone. That was the end of that.

POW CAMP

I really liked being a radio guy. Throughout all the patrols, I got to talk to quite a few helicopter pilots, as well as jet pilots and tank commanders. I knew where and when we were going before anyone else did. There were times on patrols when guys would look to me to see if there were signs of us going back. I could hear the platoon leader talking to headquarters, and I knew if we were heading back or continuing on. I would smile to everyone and they knew we were going back, or I would make a hand gesture, thumbs down, if we were continuing on. I sort of liked that.

We kept rotating from patrols and ambushes back to the bridge. Sometimes they sent us to the prisoner of war camp. That job was great. All we had to do was sit there and guard, but nobody ever moved around. The prisoners weren't going anywhere; they just lazed around and smoked cigarettes. They never seemed to talk to each other. During the day we would lie around, catch up on sleep, write home, and play with our bayonets, and we got real good throwing at targets. Being at the POW camp was the Marine Corps's way of saying "take a break." We never had a problem with any of the POWs.

There was a tower there that nobody used. We would go up there from time to time and smoke a joint because no one could smell it up there. At one time or another, we all went up those steps, and when we were done smoking, it seemed like five hundred steps coming down. I was a little afraid of heights, so I was the last one who came down from the tower. I was slow and I hugged those stairs all the way down. Once the other guys got to the ground, they just lay there on the ground under the tower, waiting to laugh at me as I came down. They just lay there, pointing and laughing at me. They were real assholes. Anyhow, we stayed at the camp for about one week and then went back to the compound, back to the patrols and ambushes.

It seemed like we had a lot of injuries as time went by. A lot of guys who were wounded never came back. When some guy came back with a new uniform and new boots, he told us how wonderful the hospital was and how good the food was.

I had been in country now for about four months. I was promoted to lance corporal, and I really felt like this squad was my family. We all felt like that, and we continued to grow ever closer. We all knew each other's friends and family. We all had nicknames. Mine was JJ, and that was fine with me. We were told we were going out the next day, daytime patrol.

THE TOMMY GUN

T he next morning, after roll call and breakfast, we lined up for departure. We were told that a lieutenant would be going out with us. We didn't know who he was or why he was going out with us, but away we went, and he walked right behind me. One thing stood out on this guy, and it was pretty obvious: he had an old French tommy gun strapped around his neck, nice and clean. He also had his helmet strap snapped on. The first thing they had told me at 2/1 was not to use that strap because if you encountered a booby trap it would take your head off.

We were about one-third of the way through our patrol when the lieutenant told us to stop. He said he saw movement in a tree line to our right, but Harrison, on point, said nobody was there. And Flaky Jake backed him up. The lieutenant told me to contact Golf Company, so I called back and asked Golf Company to hold. The lieutenant told me to give him the radio, and he told Golf Company that he had observed suspicious movement in a tree line and requested that we open fire on that tree line. They told us to wait. We started looking at each other, shrugging our shoulders. Then Golf Company told him to go ahead. We were all looking at one another, wondering what the hell was going on.

He handed the radio back to me and told the squad leader to get the squad to aim at that tree line and spray the area with gunfire. We all knew at that point that this lieutenant was determined to shoot his tommy gun, so the squad leader told us all to open fire, and we did.

I took out my .45 pistol and shot two or three rounds. I looked at the lieutenant; he was really getting into shooting that weapon. He had all tracers loaded in his clips, and I could see all his bullets being fired. His tommy gun was really bad; it was shooting all over the place. Everyone fired a full clip into that tree line and stopped, but he kept putting clip after clip into that tommy gun as we all smiled at each other. He didn't seem to notice that everybody had stopped firing.

You should have seen the way he held that weapon when he was firing it. It was a sight to behold. By now everybody in the world knew where we were, and we didn't like that at all because our element of surprise was gone, so we had to be extra careful now. That's exactly what we did. We knew if there were any VC around they would try to pick us off or shoot mortars at us. I called back to Golf Company and told them we found nothing and we were proceeding on patrol, over and out.

As we walked on patrol, he held that weapon so tightly I could see his white knuckles. As I walked through the rice paddies, it was the first time I felt like we were the hunted. I could tell by the body language of the other guys that they felt the same way. We went through our whole course and headed back to the compound. Once inside the compound, the lieutenant said good-bye and good luck to us all. We never saw him again. But all night long we pretended to be that lieutenant, and we would stand the way he stood, with his legs apart, with that stupid tommy gun, pretending to shoot each other.

THE REUNION

Patrols, basically. That's all we did. If we went out on nighttime ambushes, we would sleep all day, and when we went out on daytime patrols, we would sleep all night. Patrols were always pre-planned and for the most part covered quite a few miles, some longer and some shorter. Patrols would always start out next to the guards that were in a bunker next to the trail that zigzagged through the barbed wire. We would all line up in our designated positions. Our squad leader would tell us to lock and load and would then tell the point man which direction to go. Then we would all start out. I would radio back to Golf Company that we were leaving the compound, over and out. As we passed the guards on duty, we would exchange good-byes. We were each about six to eight feet behind one another as we zigzagged through the wire toward the tree line.

Once we got to the tree line, our squad leader would tell the point man which direction to go, and then we were off. Harrison had become an excellent point man. He was very professional in the way he used his point stick and his sense of direction. You had to do a lot of things at once. You had to know which direction to go and watch where you walk, look for booby traps, and be aware of the enemy, all at once.

Then there was the cover man. He had to make sure the point man was heading in the right direction, but most importantly, he was protecting the point man. His name was Mike Moore, and he was from Washington, DC. One night we were kidding around in our hooch when Mike did something stupid, and somebody said, "Hey, that's Flaky Jake." So that name stuck to him. Flaky Jake was the shortest guy in the squad, but he wanted to be the cover man. I had no idea how good he would become at that position. He was great with a shotgun, which he called Bernadette. He was also the best shooter with a grenade launcher, a.k.a. blooper or M79.

Then there was the squad leader, who would guide us very accurately through rice paddies and thick jungle brush from one checkpoint to another while making sure his squad was alert and professional in every way.

Next in line was myself with the radio. I always walked behind my squad leader. I was always number four, and behind me was the rest of the squad. We had a guy named George Grey, a.k.a. Weasel, and everybody wanted him to walk behind them because he was the oldest guy in the squad and a sound marine with any weapon.

Then we had a guy named Bill Tangway, from Detroit. We had a guy named Dave Kitchen, from Kansas, as quiet as they come, who rarely spoke but had keen eyesight. He would snap his finger and point to somebody working in a rice paddy or walking on a dike quite a distance away. David was gifted, and we knew it.

The size of the squad was always different. Sometimes our squad consisted of six or seven guys. Sometimes our squad had nine guys. Very rarely did we have more than nine. Sometimes, due to injuries, squads would be down to five guys, so they would borrow guys from other squads until they got replacements. Most patrols would have three checkpoints, and every time we reached a checkpoint I would radio back to Golf Company and continue on. After we reached our last checkpoint, we would head back to the compound. Once we were in view of the compound we would stop, and I would radio to Golf that we had reached the tree line. At that point Golf Company told us to come on in, and that was how our patrols operated all the time.

The next day we went out on daytime patrols. There was only so much water you could carry with you. Everybody usually carried two canteens, and some guys had three. You could carry only so much weight with all your ammo and grenades and flak jacket and helmet and weapon. That particular day on patrol it was extremely hot, and after a few hours, we ran out of water. We were standing and walking through rice paddies. They were loaded with water, but that water was covered with Agent Orange chemicals. Even though we had quinine tablets, we were reluctant to drink it.

After a while it became apparent that we had to drink that water from the rice paddies. So we filled up our canteens and dropped the quinine tablets in, and we had to wait one hour for the water to be purified. Still, nobody wanted to drink it, but it was hot and we were thirsty. We knew we had to drink it at that point. Harrison stopped and held his stick up in the air, pointing to a group of amphibs heading toward us. An amphib was a craft that carried different kinds of equipment and traveled in water and on land. They were heading right for us. We counted five of them, one behind the other.

We started waving our rifles to get their attention, and they saw us and stopped. We exchanged hellos and asked them where they were headed, and they told us they were going to the 2/1 compound. We told them they were headed in the right direction. We asked if they had any spare water, and the lead driver said they didn't have enough to share. Then the convoy started to pull away. We stood there watching as they passed by, and when the fourth amphib got to where we were standing, it stopped, and the driver told the other amphibs to stop, and oh my God, it was Butch, the guy I'd joined the Marine Corps with.

I was shocked to see him, and he was shocked to see me. I had so much to say to him. I thought he looked great. We kept shaking hands and yelling at one another and laughing. Boy, it was great to see Butch. We stared at each other, knowing we were short on time. I asked him if he had any water, and he said absolutely. He went back to the rear of his vehicle and brought back a five-gallon container and told us the drinks were on him.

I could hear the lead driver yelling at Butch, telling him to stop fucking around. I could hear the other drivers gunning their engines. Butch told me not to worry about them, but he was pissed off because his leader was threatening him. Butch said he had to go, shook my hand, and told us to just dump the container. Then they took off.

I was still shocked as they drove away, but everybody was dumping their canteens out and thanking me. That water was delicious. It was hot as hell, but nobody complained. Just for the record, Butch told me where he was stationed, and a couple weeks later I was able to find him. We had a couple of hours together; it was nice.

SICK BAY

The next day our corpsman, Doc Menard, caught me scratching my feet, and he told me to take my socks off. He said that I had a bad case of ringworm. I don't know how I got it. There were big red circles all over my feet, which were bloody from my scratching. He was pissed off because I had said nothing about them. He told me not to wear boots for ten days and no patrols, either.

We all liked Doc. He and all the other corpsmen were held in high respect because we knew he was the guy who would save your life if and when you needed him.

He got me a pair of canvas slippers and gave me cotton swabs with medication, telling me to use the medication every eight hours. As a result I got a real needling from the guys, and they said that I would do anything to get out of the bush. Those guys were just jealous because I was lying on my cot, healing my feet that never stopped itching, and I was forbidden to scratch them.

When it came time for those guys to go on patrol, I would ask them if there was anything I could do for them while they were gone. I didn't know why they cursed at me. To this day I still don't know why they cursed so much at me.

It didn't take long for our platoon sergeant to find out that I was doing nothing, but I was healing, and he said, "Bullshit." He told me that I was going on guard duty and shithouse detail. The next morning I was on guard duty, and I saw Bravo Squad line up for patrol. I stood there in the bunker talking to Harrison, and I told him, "Good luck, and please be careful."

I then heard our squad leader telling everybody to lock and load. Harrison started out, and one by one the guys walked past me. We would exchange words, from "good luck" to "God bless" and "Semper fi." I watched my squad as they zigzagged through the barbed wire and then through the open field, approaching the tree line. I felt funny not being with them. It was a strange feeling as I watched them disappear into the tree line one by one.

As the day went by, I could see squads from other companies going out on patrol at different times. Our compound was round, and each company had its own sector to patrol, and that's exactly what we did. Echo Company, Foxtrot Company, Golf Company, and Hotel Company did the same thing every day, 24-7. When a patrol was coming back, they would come to our bunker and tell us which direction they would come in from and when.

Being on guard duty was boring, and the hours felt like days, but I was healing, and I wasn't scratching my feet. I was waiting for Bravo Squad to return. Then I could see Harrison emerging from the tree line, and I smiled. As each one of the guys came out of that tree line, I counted them one by one. I watched as they zigzagged through the wire and came up a sand dune to my bunker. I asked Harrison for some ID, and he said something I can't repeat. I then asked all the other guys if they shit out in the bush so I didn't have to clean it up at the shithouse, and they also responded negatively. I told them I was healing, but I couldn't understand their mumbling. I was glad to see them.

When I was on nighttime guard duty, it was different. When the squads went out for a night ambush, they would line up about an hour or two before sunset, depending on the distance to their designated location. You always wanted to get to your ambush site at sunset or as close as you could get to it as the sun was going down. Even if you got to your spot early and the sun was still up, you would walk in a circle, never letting the enemy know where you were setting up, if they were watching. When you could barely see where you were going, you'd set up the ambush site. The squad leader knew exactly where his squad would be placed for the night. That was the time to head for your site and settle in. The squad leader would stop and pair his men. Sometimes he put two together, sometimes three depending on the size of the squad. At that time you would dig in and get comfortable. After that there was no talking, no smoking—period.

While still on duty, I figured those guys were just getting settled in, and I wished them nothing but the best. As I was thinking of them, I could hear and see all the flares being sent up all around the compound. It was real dark, and everything was quiet. All you could hear was the sound of flares being set off. Those flares traveled pretty far up, depending on what angle you used when you set one off. We had a box of flares in our bunker, and at any time you thought you saw something or heard something, you were allowed to send up a flare. An average flare goes straight up about two hundred or three hundred yards, pops out on a parachute, and slowly drifts back to earth. I was surprised by how bright the flares were. They lasted about two minutes, and that was plenty of time to see if there was any movement anywhere.

While in the bunker, I would look up into the sky, and I would see these gunships far off in the distance using tracer bullets, a sight that I'll never forget. After the tracers stopped hitting the ground, about thirty seconds later I would hear what sounded like a zipper—the sound of all those bullets hitting the ground. Sometimes that would go on all night long. They called that gunship Puff, and I wouldn't want to be on the receiving end of that gunship. I stared at the stars. I had never seen so many and such brightness.

All night long someone was always coming by, making sure we were not asleep. If they caught you asleep, you were in deep shit. I was relieved around two o'clock in the morning, and I went back to my empty hooch and lay down on my cot, saying a prayer for Bravo Squad, and went to sleep.

Then it was sunup, and I heard those guys come back, and I lay there counting each one as they came into the hooch. That day I was on shithouse detail, and what you did when you were on that detail was lift the back door of the shithouse up and take out half barrels and put in empty barrels before closing the door. Then you took those barrels to a designated spot and burned them. That wasn't a good job, but I was still healing and still not itching.

That night I was back on guard duty around six o'clock, and we saw Alpha Squad getting ready to go out on ambush. As they went by me, I wished good luck to each and every one of them. I watched them as they disappeared into the tree line. I knew where they were going, and I wished them God's blessing.

About fifteen minutes before sundown, I saw these two marine snipers walking up to our bunker. They never said a word. Their faces were all painted, and they had big rifles with nightscopes on them. As they walked by, I said "good luck" to them, but they never answered me. I looked up at them and noticed neither of them made eye contact with me either. I never saw them speak to each other. I was told that they went out just before sunset, found a tree, climbed it, stayed up in it all night, and did what they did. I remember thinking I wouldn't want to be one of them.

CHRISTMAS

My ringworm went away, and my boots went back on, and again we were sent to Two Cal Bridge. It was Christmastime. We were all on duty, checking IDs and looking for anything suspicious, anything that could be used by the enemy. We also did a lot of swimming while we were there. A lot of kids used to come up to us on bikes, always bugging us to buy whatever they were selling. Some of the kids were aggressive in trying to sell their stuff, always cursing, while others would try to cheat you by not giving you the correct change or giving you nine joints in a bag instead of ten. They all seemed to be underfed. They had baskets on their bikes, and those baskets were full of different stuff they sold: bottles of Coca-Cola, watered-down whiskey, beer that was awful, and even marijuana—ten joints and a bag for a dollar.

There were also a lot of senior women walking by, carrying what looked like a hundred pounds of stuff on their shoulders. It was amazing how they did it. They had long boards on their shoulders, and on each end hung a container full of whatever they were carrying. They walked to a rhythm. The board would bend and the containers would bounce with every other step. It was natural for them. A way of life. We used to be in awe as we watched a seventy-year-old woman carry so much weight. We also used to watch women eat lice out of each other's hair. We saw that all that time, and they thought nothing of it. In fact they looked like they enjoyed it.

Most of the civilians never spoke to us or looked up at us; they just kept on walking until we stopped them. We didn't speak Vietnamese, but we had learned a few words to communicate with the civilians.

A big military truck stopped at the bridge, and an officer got out and started yelling to everybody in the back of the truck to get out. About a dozen marines jumped out of the back wearing clean new uniforms. We all looked at one another, wondering what was going on. The major told us that we were going to the USO show and his soldiers would take over for us at the bridge until we got back. We started laughing in disbelief, but the major yelled, "What are you waiting for? Come on; let's go." He told us "Merry Christmas" and said Bob Hope was waiting for us. We asked the major if he had the right squad. He said he had orders to relieve us at the bridge and escort us to the USO show immediately. We started laughing as the new guys took our positions. We all said, "Let's roll."

So we jumped in the back of the truck in two seconds flat. We were all high-fiving and yelling like crazy. The truck driver revved his engine as he turned around with the major sitting next to him. We took off, heading north—*here we come, Danang.* We were filthy. At every checkpoint the major would get out of the truck and show the guards some type of pass or orders. They would open up the road gates and let us by. We would salute the MPs as we passed.

The closer we got to the show, the more checkpoints we encountered, and more and more soldiers would stare at us. We felt funny as these other soldiers kept stopping and staring. We felt like outcasts, misfits. The truck driver and the major were wearing clean uniforms. We were having a real problem getting through checkpoints. The MPs didn't like us going in with our weapons. Everyone seemed to be afraid of us. The major was showing the MPs our orders, and he was clearly pissed off. We watched as the major pointed to us and then pointed toward Danang, holding our orders. We spent a lot of time going through all these check-points, and it was taking us longer and longer to pass through each one. We were all disappointed because of the delay, but the major was furious.

We finally made it to the gates of where the USO show was underway. The MPs refused to let us go in with our weapons. Again we watched as the major and the MPs went at it. The MPs got on the radio, and after what seemed like half an hour, the MPs pulled the major aside and said no weapons, period. As we sat in the back of the truck, the major walked up and said he was doing the best he could to get us inside. All these soldiers were walking all around us, looking at us like we had done something wrong. All of them were slowing up and listening to what was going on.

By that time the major was red-faced and clearly mad. He came to the back of the truck and said, "They cannot take your weapons, but we are not allowed inside with them. Exit the truck and leave your weapons here, and the driver will stay and watch over them. You have my word." That was fine with us—no problem.

All eight of us jumped out of the truck, and the major told us that he would also stay with our weapons and apologized for all the delays. He told us to come back to the truck when the show was over. Then he told us to hurry up. There were so many soldiers there. Everywhere we went they would stare at us and get out of our way. We felt funny. But we couldn't do anything about that.

The show was half-over, and we were in the back of the back. All we could see were the backs of people's heads. We couldn't even see the stage, but we could hear the loudspeakers, and that was about it. It sounded like people were dancing. We all stood there for about five minutes, and we unanimously decided that it was no fun at all. So we thought we would try to make phone calls. We saw all the signs saying, "Call home. Free." So we headed for the phones.

When we got to the phone lines, there must have been ten thousand soldiers in each line. There was no way we could stand in those lines, and we all knew it. We tried in vain to ask the MPs if we could somehow get to the fronts of the lines because we only had a short amount of time, but they said to forget it. No way.

Well, we couldn't see the show, and we couldn't call home, so we decided to go to the PX, a military store where food and drinks, cigarettes, clothing, and toiletries could be purchased. Every soldier had a PX card. You got one every month. That card listed what you were entitled to and how much you were allowed to purchase. We wanted booze, but that would be a problem. Our PX cards, normally listing "Liquor two bottles," were blacked out because of who we were. We were grunts; we were not allowed to buy any liquor ever. We also didn't have enough money because whenever you were out of the compound you never carried any money. A couple bucks, maybe, but that was it. Between the eight of us, we only had a few dollars.

We stood there in front of the PX, listening to the show going on in the background. We knew we were running out of time, so what the hell were we going to do? We started asking soldiers walking past if they could help us out and buy liquor for us. One by one they veered away from us, saying no and telling us to find somebody else. Finally we cornered this air force guy. He was a young airman, and he said he would help us. We all looked at each other with elation. He said he didn't drink, so he could get us two bottles of whatever we wanted. We told him we didn't have a lot of money, and he said not to worry; he would pay for the rest of it. Boy, were we happy.

We all started yelling what we wanted, but there was no way we could get eight bottles, so we picked the two oldest guys to go in with the airman and get something good. They went in, picked out what they wanted, and came out smiling and laughing. They were in there for five long minutes. We stood in a circle around the air force guy, asking what kind of booze we got, and he showed us a bottle of rum and a bottle of bourbon. People were walking by thinking we were doing something to him. We all shook his hand and thanked him. He said, "Merry Christmas, marines," and showed us his PX card. He pointed out where they had punched two holes on his card next to the word "Liquor." Then he smiled.

The show was breaking up, and we started to head back to the truck. We knew we had to cover up our Christmas presents, but that was no problem. We got back on the truck, and the major asked us how we liked the show. We told the major we'd had a wonderful time. We started back. It took us a long time to get through the traffic. We were all smiles in the back of that truck. We hoped we had enough Coca-Cola at the bridge.

Finally we made it to the bridge, and the major said, "Good-bye and good luck." He loaded his guys back on the truck, and they took off. Then we had our own Christmas party that night. Our first toast of the night was to Bob Hope for putting on a wonderful show.

OPERATION

We left the bridge and went back to base. We were told we were going on an operation the next day. This time we would be traveling with a company of South Vietnamese soldiers. We called them "ARVNs" as they were from the Army of the Republic of Vietnam. We didn't like or trust them at all. I guess it was just their culture or something; it was just the way they looked. Same size, same hair; they walked and talked just like the VC soldiers. They would always walk together holding hands, and it seemed like every one of them smoked cigarettes, one after the other. They had a reputation of dropping their weapons and running away when they were fired upon. We were not looking forward to being on their side. All of us felt the same, but onward we went.

An operation took a lot of planning. There was a lot of preparation, most of all coordination, by the whole battalion. We took off early that day and were flown out to a specific destination, chopper after chopper. We must've looked like a swarm of locusts from the ground. As we landed, we ran out of the choppers and through the elephant grass just as fast as we could, making sure we were far away from the chopper blades. We then got down on one knee, squad by squad, trying to make some type of formation. Now we had the Second Battalion landing all at once, plus the company of ARVNs.

We all panned out—Echo Company, Foxtrot Company, Golf Company, ARVNs, Hotel Company, and the scouts—trying to make one straight line. Golf Company was just about set. We had Fox Company on our left and the ARVNs on our right. Golf Company had the First Platoon on the left, Second Platoon in the middle, and the Third Platoon on the right. Our platoon was set up with Alpha Squad left, Bravo Squad center, and Charlie Squad on the right because the Second Platoon was in the middle of Gulf Company. Bravo Squad was in the middle of the Second Platoon.

Our company commander traveled with us. He told me that my call sign that day would be Golf Company, and I was to stay with him at all times. Our company commander was all business. We kept looking over at the ARVNs. I saw Flaky Jake with his shotgun on his hip, smirking at the ARVNs, shaking his head. After about ten minutes, we were told to move out slow and easy. Everyone was saying, "Stay abreast of each other" and "Don't clump up on each other."

Our orders that day were simple: Search and destroy booby-traps, bunkers, caches of any kind. We were also flushing out the enemy. We were always on guard for snipers. But it was next to impossible to see them until they opened fire, and when they did open fire they would get off maybe two or three shots, where we would send back about two thousand rounds, so they were very careful when and where they took their shots. The VC were very smart; they were men and women, young and old. We were in their backyard. They knew the area well. Basically we were on a human hunt, and so were they. We kept looking over at the ARVNs. I was dying to know how they'd react to contact when we encountered the enemy. Would they drop their weapons and run away?

Our operation was going pretty smoothly. We had a lot of fire-power. Not only did we have five companies, but each company had its own M60 gun squad and its own mortar squad. A gun squad consisted of three or four guys. One guy carried the M60 machine gun. Another guy carried the tripods, and the other guy or guys carried the ammo. Those M60s did a lot of damage. A mortar squad had three or four guys; one carried the mortar, one carried the firing plate and tripods, and one carried ammo.

I was following my captain all over the place. We would go over to the First Platoon, making sure everybody was online, and then we would run over to the Third Platoon, constantly checking and making sure that each company was in order. There wasn't much chatter on the radio. It seemed like nobody worried about anything except staying online. We all knew there was a reason they had placed us in that sector, and we figured that intelligence knew somebody was in the area.

As we walked along, we checked everything. We could see a village up ahead and heard yelling. Somebody had seen us coming, and I guessed they were yelling, "Here come the marines." Then we heard another yell, farther away, probably saying the same thing, warning the VC that we were coming. There was nothing we could do about that.

When we reached the village, we couldn't identify who was yelling. If there were any VC there, they would have been gone, but maybe not. As we stood there, we would talk among ourselves that we wouldn't be surprised at all if they were sitting right there basket-weaving or something else. The villagers would just do whatever they were doing; they would act like we weren't even there.

Our captain told me to contact the ARVN Company and asked for a translator to come over and talk to the villagers. At the same time, we were checking everything in that village. Again I saw the women eating the lice from one another's heads. It seemed that no matter where we went I saw that. I thought it was odd and disgusting. The translator showed up, and he started asking all kinds of questions, but he wasn't getting many answers, and I could see he was getting upset. We checked everybody's IDs, and everything seemed to be in order.

The translator said that the villagers had no knowledge of any VC in the area, and each of our squad leaders reported that nothing suspicious has been found. I was told to radio back to 2/1 that the village was clean. We were about three hours into our operation, and a couple minutes later 2/1 told us to move out. There were lots of helicopters flying all over our heads. It was a roar of rotors heading in the same direction as us. Then, out in front of us, we could hear the helicopters opening fire. Bullets galore.

All of a sudden the radio was chattering like crazy; everybody wanted to know what those helicopters were firing at. Those helicopters reported seeing VC carrying weapons and running away from our position. Our mission was to flush any combatants out and destroy all bunkers, caves, caches, holes, and tree perches. The operation that we were employing was doing its job. The VC had left quite a few booby traps for us all along the way, so we had to stop and destroy them. Sometimes they were hidden so well that we had casualties.

We got orders from 2/1 to pick up the pace but not get in front of anybody else. Our operation was acting like a door that was closing, chasing the VC straight toward a river. It wasn't very long, once we left that village, before we began taking incoming. We were sprayed by bullets and pounded by mortars. I was dying to see what the ARVNs were doing, and they stood their ground. I kept looking over, waiting and waiting, but I saw them firing back right alongside us. Nobody ran.

A band of VC was held up in a tree line about five hundred yards away. My captain told me to radio the First and Third platoons and tell them to hold up. We then got word from 2/1 for everyone to stop. It seemed like the whole line was being pounded from that tree line. Then the captain asked me for the radio headset, and I heard him ask headquarters if there was any air support available. Headquarters immediately called back and confirmed that there was a jet available in our area and that he would give us a flyby. At the same time, those VC in that tree line just kept letting us have it, everything they had. They would not stop, and as much as they fired at us, we fired right back at them. We had quite a few wounded marines, and we got them out quickly.

Headquarters called and told us that the jet pilot was switching over to our frequency, and as soon as he did we would direct him to that tree line. Bullets and mortars were flying everywhere, and I could hear the jet pilot calling for Golf Company and asking us to please come in. It was hard to hear him with all the shooting and rotors around me. He said his call name was Bluebird. I told the captain that the jet pilot was on the line and his call sign was Bluebird. The captain grabbed my headset, and I heard him welcome the pilot. He asked the pilot if he could help him out a little, and I saw the captain smile. Then they exchanged words, and the captain handed the headset back to me.

He went over and got a red smoke grenade and tried to tell everyone to stop firing, but with all the incoming and everybody shooting, the M60s going and the mortars popping, it was impossible. Again he yelled, "Everyone cease fire." Now everybody was running to the guy next to him, telling him to cease fire.

Things settled down, but we were still getting lots of incoming. All of a sudden all of the choppers took off. The captain again asked for my headset. He then threw the smoke grenade into an open field, and I heard him ask the pilot if he saw the red smoke, and the pilot confirmed that he did. The captain then told him to go five hundred yards north from the red smoke at the tree line. I could hear the jet coming loud and fast.

He dropped a napalm bomb right on that tree line. Then everybody started yelling and screaming and jumping up and down. I heard the captain tell the pilot that was the spot, and the pilot said, "Stand by for another run." He came around and again hit the throttle, and he swooped right down and dropped at least three or four napalm bombs. We were close to where they exploded. We felt the heat, and the sound was deafening, but that was the end of the incoming. As I listened to the headset, I heard the pilot say he was glad to help, over and out. We then took a breather. We all just sat there watching the trees burn up, and the smell was awful.

We got a call from 2/1, and they told us to start humping again, so we all stood up and started moving. But the ARVNs would not get up, so we stopped, and our captain radioed headquarters and told them that the ARVNs were not moving. The captain and I went over to the ARVNs, and their captain said that his men were tired and needed a longer rest and they were not done eating. I thought it was funny, but the captain didn't.

The captain radioed back to headquarters that the ARVNs needed more time before we could move out. Headquarters told us to let them know when the ARVNs were ready. Our captain told Golf Company to take a break but be ready to go after about a half hour. The ARVNs' captain told us they were ready to go, so our captain called headquarters and said we were ready to start out again. So we did.

We cautiously approached that tree line. All you could smell was sulfur and wood; whatever had been there was gone. It was a smell like no other. I had mixed feelings because the VC had been incinerated that way, but I tried to stay focused on the job at hand. We kept on going in a straight line, very slowly, and then one of our guys started looking over at the ARVNs, talking about the lingering smell, the heat, and cursing like crazy at the ARVNs. He just snapped and started shooting at the sun.

Everybody hit the deck, so the captain told me to radio headquarters and tell them that one of our guys had a heat stroke and was shooting in thin air. Then I heard the captain yelling for someone to take his weapon from him, lay him down on the ground, and pour water over his head and chest, which he did. We took a five-minute break. When we started out again, the guy who did the shooting seemed really embarrassed. But he seemed to be OK. He was apologizing to everybody, but we didn't give him back his weapon.

Then we approached a large field with no trees but lots of large bushes. The captain and I were walking back and forth between the First and Third platoons. We could hear gunfire on our left side and on our right side. Then the line stopped, and we didn't know why. Then Fox Company called us and said we were holding up everybody and they wanted to know why. We were not moving. We also got a call from headquarters. The whole battalion was standing still, and the captain told me to follow him.

As we walked along the line, everybody kept pointing to the right. As we approached I could see Harrison lying on the ground. He kept saying that he should be dead over and over again. We tried talking to him, but he just kept saying "I should be dead. I should be dead." I looked at Flaky Jake, who was pointing to a grenade that was tied to a piece of bamboo. We saw that Harrison had tripped a wire. This time his stick hadn't found it. What was amazing was that the firing pin never went off, so the grenade never exploded.

Headquarters was on us to move it out, and we did, but Harrison just lay there; he wouldn't get up. As we walked away, I turned around and saw the corpsman trying to get him up. The whole battalion was up and running, everybody in line. There were a lot of helicopters buzzing around, especially the small ones called mosquitoes. They were real quick and quiet. You couldn't hear them coming until they were right on top of you. As we flushed the VC out, those mosquitoes were right on them, and as we kept walking we saw bodies all over.

During that operation we discovered many caches, lots of bunkers, and we destroyed them all. That operation lasted a few days. We were told that headquarters couldn't be happier. As for the company of ARVNs, well, we knew that they didn't run away when things got hard, but we still didn't like them. After we split up with the ARVNs, we all talked about them. We all agreed they just could not be trusted. Harrison was taken back to the battalion area, but he had a faraway stare now. His voice was much lower, and he was always praising God. They found a job for him at headquarters, and I got to see him whenever we were in camp.

THE ISLAND

Our platoon was sent to a small patch of ground called No Name Island with orders to dig in and hold it till notified. We knew another platoon had just been beaten up there. The foxholes were already in place, but we were all uneasy being there. There was water all around it, about two or three feet deep, and elephant grass everywhere. The tree lines were about two hundred or three hundred yards away, but this place was to be our home. We would run patrols all day. All three squads would take turns patrolling while the guns and mortar squad stayed on the island.

Things were pretty quiet most of the time. We would clean our weapons, lie there and sunbathe, shoot the shit, and wave to the choppers flying by. We would get a sniper shot every so often and at night a rocket or mortar round. At night we could see the flashes from where they were launched. Then we would return fire immediately in the direction of the flashes. The next morning we combed the area, looking for weapons and dead VC. The VC wanted us to know that they were there. They wanted us to know that they would never go away, no matter how many patrols or helicopters or anything else we had. That was why they would shoot off one or two rounds and run away; they hoped we would come right

51

after them with their booby traps set up. Sometimes we would find a North Vietnamese flag hanging in a nearby tree.

We were on that island four days when we ran out of water. I radioed back to Golf Company requesting water. A short time later, a helicopter pilot contacted us, and I picked up the radio and made contact with him. He said he was within a couple miles of our destination. We could hear the chopper coming, and it was soon circling overhead. The chopper had a net hanging under its belly with eight cans of water.

We were all waving our arms. I was on the radio, looking right at the two pilots. I told them we were thirsty. He said, "Roger, Golf Two," and bullets started hitting the helicopter. The helicopter started to wobble back and forth. I could hear the pilots yelling and cursing. Our guys started shooting at where those bullets were coming from, but the VC just kept on firing at the helicopter. The machine gunner on that chopper was firing back. The helicopter tried to turn around and go backward. I heard the pilot yell, "Let's get out of here!" That's when they cut the net and the cans dropped into the water about 150 yards away from us. That chopper disappeared, leaving a trail of smoke.

As soon as the helicopter left, the VC stopped firing, and our captain told us to cease fire. We all looked at one another and then to where those cans might be out in the water. The captain said we had to get to those cans fast. He told all three of us radio operators to take off our gear and keep our .45 pistols on. He picked another guy and told him to take off all his gear and then yelled to our cover man, Flaky Jake, to lead us out with his shotgun. He told us four guys and Jake to go out there. He told us to follow behind Jake and run to the cans of water, no talking.

My heart was pounding like crazy as we left the island. We ran as fast as we could behind Jake. I was right behind him as he waved his shotgun back and forth. The water at times came up to our waist. The elephant grass was tall and full of bugs. You couldn't see very far ahead. Everything was so quiet; we just kept running toward where we thought the cans of water were. All I could hear was the water we were splashing. We didn't know if the VC were still in the area, but we just kept running. It seemed like we would never get there.

Jake did a real good job; he got us right to the spot. Jake ran past the cans, stood there with his shotgun, looked all around, and then told us to go, go, go. I remember thinking if anything was going to happen, it would be now. We each grabbed two cans of water and started running back to the island just as fast as we could in single file. I was up front, hoping that I was heading straight for the island. If you lifted the cans of water up too high, they felt like fifty pounds each, and it slowed us down, but if you dragged the cans through the water, it was a lot easier, but that also slowed us down.

I turned around real fast and saw Jake walking backward, waving his shotgun back and forth. The bugs were eating us up, but I couldn't swat them. We were halfway back to the island and hadn't taken any incoming. But it was so quiet that the water splashing was all I heard. I tried to keep my head down, saying prayers. We just kept dragging those cans through the water till we got back to the island. I felt like there was a target on my back. We were about twenty yards away from the island.

The guys on the island saw we were out of breath, so they came out and helped us. The four of us lay there on the ground, gasping for air, except Jake. He came walking out of the water, smiling, just patting his shotgun. He said that Bernadette had taken good care of us. He loved his shotgun. He just sat right down, got a cloth, and started to wipe off Bernadette.

POW CAMP

We left No Name Island and went back to base. After eight days of eating C rations, we were looking forward to some hot chow. Actually, eating out of cans wasn't that bad. My personal preference was spaghetti and meatballs. I hated the ham and eggs.

They looked like vomit in a can. We were all glad to get back to base and felt a lot better after a good night's rest.

We had roll call in the morning, and then they told us to fall out. My brother Jack was always sending me music tapes, so I would find someone in the compound with a reel-to-reel tape machine and ask him if I could use it for a while. That was never a problem. If he was using the machine at the time he would tell me when to come back. The guys loved it when I played the tapes in the hooch. He sent all the newest hits back in the world. In between songs my brother would ask how Bravo Squad was doing. Then someone would yell out, "We are doing good, brother! Play more music!" Then we all laughed.

Sometimes I got a tape from my mom, but I didn't want those guys listening to her worrying about me. That tape was for me only. All the other guys would just sit around cleaning their weapons or just snoozing.

We were told that we were going back to the POW camp. We loved going there. Sometimes I think of how crazy we were when we played the game of chicken. There was nothing else to do at that camp, so all we did all day was play with our bayonets, and we were all pretty good throwing at targets. Then we would play that stupid game called Chicken, which involved two guys, and both guys would face each other, about four feet apart, with their legs spread far apart. Then one of the guys would throw his bayonet between the other guy's legs, and that guy would move his foot right next to the bayonet. Then it was his turn to throw the bayonet back between the other guy's legs. Then he would move his foot over to that bayonet. Everyone would just sit around and watch and yell. Then the other would pick the knife up without moving his foot and throw it back between the other guy's feet.

This went on and on until their feet were about two inches apart. That's where things got crazy. Everybody got real quiet; nobody moved. Most of the guys would watch the other guy throw that bayonet between those two inches. They would close their eyes, including me, and sometimes a guy would chicken out and jump in the air as the bayonet was thrown. Then everybody would yell "chicken!" We must've been crazy to play that game. I am surprised that no one ever really got hurt.

We found out there was a Green Beret camp right next door, so we wandered over there to take a look. Five of us went in, took a look around, and we noticed how nice their quarters were. They had big soft beds; they all seemed to be just sitting around. One of the Green Berets told us to go take a look at their club. So we took a walk over and went inside the club. It was nice and looked like a bar from home. It was well stocked, and they had hamburgers. We asked if we could buy something, and they said sure, so we all sat at the bar and ordered drinks, and we couldn't help but notice all the bags of snacks. We all just sat there smiling. We quickly ran out of money, but we vowed to come back. Then we headed back to the POW camp. We couldn't wait to tell the other guys what we had found and to get more money. We were not permitted to drink alcohol, but over at that camp they never said a word.

I remember one time we really got drunk. They asked us to leave. As we walked out of their camp, we saw the Berets sitting in their barracks. We started to mouth off to them, saying, "Why are you guys just sitting around? Why aren't you guys out in the bush?" We just kept on saying that out loud. That was a mistake. They started to come out of their barracks, yelling at us, and then a fistfight broke out. Then the MPs showed up, and they threw us out. They never reported us. We ruined a great place.

The POW camp was in between the Green Beret camp and an army camp, and at night four of the guys in our squad were sent out to be in an LP, a listening post about fifty yards out in front of the army camp. It was a rather large foxhole, and we would go out there about twenty minutes before sunset. As we walked through the wire, we would see the army guys sitting in the towers with their radios on. Then we would go to the LP, set up our claymore mines, get settled in, and stay out there till sunrise. Then we'd pick up our claymores and head back over to the POW camp.

We would take turns going out at night. I went almost all the time because of the radio. We could never understand why they sent us out there to that LP. We thought the army should handle it. It was always quiet out there, and sometimes you could hear the music playing from the guard tower at the army camp behind us.

One night we were heading out to the LP, and as we walked through the barbed wire, we looked up at the tower. A couple of army guys waved to us as we proceeded down to our oversized foxhole. We set up our claymore mines. Those mines would help protect us if we needed them. Now we just settled in and watched the sun go down. I always called Golf Company to tell them we were in position. From time to time I would call and ask for a radio check. That's something that I did a lot. It gave me something to do. I always liked to check the radio to make sure it was working properly.

We didn't talk a lot out there because it was just so quiet. We would whisper to one another from time to time, but our job was to sit in that foxhole and listen for any enemy movement. You would hear the sounds of cans and bottles being thrown into containers from the camp. We would laugh and wish it was us doing the throwing.

After midnight that night, we got a call from Golf Company saying that a group of NVA soldiers had been spotted heading in our direction, and they were moving fast. Golf Company kept calling, asking if we saw or heard anything. I kept telling them "negative." We started to talk to each other. We were nervous. One by one we each took turns telling each other what we were going to do in life if we ever survived Nam. I don't remember what those other guys said, but I will never forget what I said that night. I told them if I got out of this place I would never complain. I would marry my girlfriend, Marilyn; have a small family; live in a small house; get a steady job; and live my life the best I could.

After we were all done saying what we would do if we survived, we waited. I turned around. I could see the guard towers filling up with soldiers. I could hear them locking and loading their weapons. We could hear movement in front of us. I called Golf Company and told them that we'd made visual contact. At the same time, someone behind us shot off flares. We could see the NVA soldiers running toward us, and then they made a sharp left. There were quite a few of them, and then all hell broke loose.

We shot off our claymores and fired everything we had. It looked like we got a couple of them from the claymores, but the rest kept running away from us.

The army guys were firing from behind us, and then one of our guys got shot in the ass. Then we realized some of the bullets that were being fired behind us were too low. I grabbed my radio, and we all jumped to the other side of the foxhole to get away from friendly fire. I called Golf Company and told them we needed a corpsman. I asked them to call the army guys behind us to remind them that we were out there in the LP. Meanwhile, our wounded guy was cursing up a storm about being shot in the ass. We put bandages on him and told him help was on the way.

We could barely see the NVA soldiers from the flares, and that fast they were out of sight. As we lay outside the foxhole, we reminded ourselves not to move. The flares were still going off. Everybody started yelling, "Cease fire." Golf Company called to say help was on the way. Sure enough, we saw guys with a stretcher zigzagging through the wire. We started yelling for the corpsman, letting them know where we were. They took our wounded away, and the three of us stayed out there till dawn. When the sun came up, we picked up our claymores and made sure Charlie was dead. Somebody got two of them.

We were pissed off about what had happened, but we understood how it had happened. When we came back through the wire, we didn't see a soul. We wanted to look at somebody, but the towers were empty.

AMBUSH

We left the POW camp and went back to base. We were told we were going out on a night ambush. Our ambush site was about a mile or so away from the base. So we left the compound about one hour or so before sunset. We made our way slow and easy to our checkpoint, and we set up our ambush site. Everything was quiet.

It was a little after midnight when all of a sudden we heard a lot of gunshots coming from the battalion compound. We saw flares going up like crazy. I could hear all the commotion on the radio, and all the guys were whispering to me, "What the hell is going on back there?" I told them it sounded like the base was being attacked.

We could see the sky lighting up from all the explosions, and the blasts got louder and louder. I kept the radio up to my ear. I listened to all the chatter coming from Golf Company. I could hear the guys in the bunkers yelling for reinforcements because the VC were coming through the wire. We could see the flares going up as fast as they could get them off. As the gunfire got louder and louder, the guys around me kept looking at me, wanting to know what the hell was happening. I told them 2/1 was under attack. This went on for about twenty minutes, and then everything was quiet.

I could hear Golf Company asking if there were any VC inside the wire. The sky was still lit up with flares, and it stayed lit for about an hour, and then nothing. I stayed on the radio, and it was definite: The base had been under attack. All I could hear was Golf Company asking about the situations at each bunker, and each bunker kept reporting one by one, "No movement." Whatever had happened back there, we'd missed out on it. After a while the radio was quiet.

We stayed out there till dawn and then got up, stretched, picked up our gear, and headed back to the compound. We were dying to know what had happened, and I made sure to tell Golf Company that we would be nearing the base and from what direction we would be coming from. As we got in eyesight of the compound, again I called Golf Company to tell them again that Golf Two Bravo was coming in, over and out.

As we got closer, we could see all these bodies hung up in the barbed wire. We started to walk real slowly, and we almost came to a stop. We just kept looking at each other and shaking our heads. It was a hell of a sight. As we walked toward the bunker, we started counting bodies, and we counted eighteen. These were just the ones in front of Golf Company. As we passed them one by one, we noticed how many tourniquets they had on them; they were every three inches on their arms and legs. We were saying it was suicidal.

As we started walking through the wire, we were now looking at the bodies face-to-face, and some of them were really shot up bad; some were decapitated men and women. We saw these two guys standing next to one another, straight up, just stuck there in the barbed wire, and you could see white powder hanging from their noses. We just kept walking, wondering why they had done what they had. To us it seemed like they knew it was suicide but they tried anyhow. They never made it halfway through. Not even close. When we got back inside the compound, we looked around, and everybody was just doing whatever it was that they were doing. It was like nothing had ever happened. We found out later it was the first anniversary of the Tet Offensive.

MAIL CALL

The Second Battalion, First Marines were located south of Danang. All four of our companies—Echo, Fox, Golf, and Hotel—were doing the same exercises every day. We would all head out in different directions and patrol all day long and every night, 24-7, all year. I didn't really get to know the other guys in the other companies even though we stayed and ate in the same compound. All of us were shuffled around all the time, and when we weren't, we were asleep.

One thing we all loved was mail call, and I must say the Marine Corps knew that. They would have mail call, and everybody would stop whatever they were doing and circle around the guy standing on an empty ammo box calling out names. I don't know about anybody else, but I hope that he called my name a hundred times.

One person I could always count on every day was my mom. I don't think she ever missed a day. I used to like to read about simple little things that meant nothing to anybody else but me. Mail used to take quite a few weeks to reach me, and sometimes when we got back from operations I would have seven or eight letters, just from my mom. My brother Jack would ask about the war and what it was like. I used to get a lot of mail from my friends, and they would talk a lot about politics, and my father was all pissed off with Washington, DC, but not my mom. She used to tell me about our dog, about church, about the neighbors, about her job, about my brothers and my father. But she always ended her letters saying that she attended the mass at six thirty every morning and lit a candle and said a special prayer for me. I never forgot that.

Mail call was a special time of day. Sometimes a guy calling out our names would yell out a name again and again, not knowing that that guy had just been shot or wounded. Everybody would become quiet and look down. Then somebody would say something, and the guy would just say OK and start calling out other names. As soon as mail call was over, we all found our own little patches of sand or boxes and just read.

We didn't have much social activity. We were not allowed to drink, and besides, we didn't have the time to do it. Most of the time, we would clean our weapons and bullshit. We had this guy with us, George Gray, and we called him the weasel because somehow or another he would always find a way to get out of going on patrol with us. He was the only married guy with us at that time. When he started talking about his wife, everybody would shut up and listen. He would sit on the edge of his cot with a letter in his hand as we were cleaning our weapons, and he would say how much he loved and missed her. He was kind of the old guy in the group. I think he was twenty-three.

He would tell us how unfortunate we were not to be married. He used to go on and on and on about his wife. And we all just listened to him as he told us how much his wife used to hug him all the time and how wonderful it was to be loved so much by someone and how they would do everything together all the time. Then he would show us her picture, saying how much he wanted to be with her. He kept saying, "You guys don't know what you're missing." I think we all felt envious.

Anyhow, everybody was entitled to an R&R (rest and relaxation) vacation after eight months of duty. The Marine Corps would give each of us a trip to a destination of our choice, free of charge. Those destinations were Australia, Thailand, Taiwan, or Hawaii. My eight months of duty was coming up soon, and I had to decide which destination to go to because it took time to get the paperwork in order. After careful thought I selected Taiwan because it was an island in the Pacific Ocean and I wanted to see the ocean.

NIGHT MEDEVAC

OUR SQUAD

W e were told that we were going out on a night ambush. This time our destination was quite a few miles away, and we would leave the compound a couple of hours before sunset. We left the compound and headed right for a village. As we got near, we could hear yelling, and we knew they were yelling that we were coming. Then we heard another yell farther away; they were passing the word along that we were coming. There was nothing we could do about that. We were concerned that the enemy now knew where we were. We would say to each other, "Hey, what kind of people are these?" We knew they were telling the enemy so they could run away or set a trap for us. None of us liked it, and it made us all feel even more unnerved as we pressed on. It slowed us down and made us think somebody was behind every bush or tree.

Again we would hear the yelling from far away and would turn around to each other, giving the thumbs up, moving ever so slowly, always fearing the snipers. Everything was so quiet I could hear George's footsteps on little pieces of bamboo on the ground behind me.

We walked into the village, and everyone was just acting normal. They pretended that we weren't even there. We looked around for anything suspicious, and as I stood there I would watch women sitting on the ground eating lice out of each other's hair. As I walked to the edge of the village, I would look out at the rice paddy and see their water buffalo being fed and bathed. They really took care of them.

It was time to move out and head to our ambush site. We still had a long way to go. We kept going, to our ambush site, and, yes, we got there with plenty of time to spare. You didn't want to get to your ambush site until the sun went down—all the way down, as someone could be watching. If you sat down too early, they would know exactly where you were, so we walked around in a big circle, knowing where we would settle in but waiting for darkness.

When it was dark enough, we set up our ambush. We put out our claymores and paired up, two or three together, depending on the size of the squad, and then dug in. We sat and waited—no talking, no smoking. All around us were the sounds of frogs, bugs, and creatures of all kinds. Sometimes after a while it sounded like an orchestra. And there was the never-ending heat.

That night there were eight of us, so we paired up in twos. It was much better to be grouped in threes, as that way you got an extra shift sleeping, but not that night. From there on out, there was total silence except for me whispering to Gulf Company, asking for a radio check. After a couple of hours you would ask your partner who wanted to sleep first. Then that person would take his shift sleeping while the other guy stood watch. Some of the shifts were two hours, and some were three. When it came time to change shifts, you would shake that person and whisper his name to get him up.

Usually everybody stayed awake till about eleven o'clock, and if everything was quiet, you would start taking shifts. That night I was with Roger, our squad leader, and I slept first, and we chose two-hour shifts. Roger woke me up at one o'clock in the morning; it was my turn to watch till three o'clock. Then I woke Roger up and went to sleep. From time to time I would check in with Golf Company, letting them know that we were OK.

It was after three o'clock when Charlie walked right into us. They opened up immediately. I was asleep then. We all jumped up and started firing back. Charlie just kept running away, and we nailed a couple of them. I then turned to Roger and realized his throat had been clipped in that initial panicked exchange. We immediately put bandages on him, and I called for a medevac. It was dangerous for the choppers at night, and the helicopter pilots didn't like to do it; we all knew that. Golf Company called back and told us they would try to get us a medevac as soon as possible, and we knew it all depended on the pilot.

As we waited we knew we had to find an open flat area for the helicopter to land in, and we were on that immediately. Golf Company called back to confirm our coordinates, and now we waited. We knew Roger was losing a lot of blood, and we started to say among ourselves that they wouldn't come, but Golf Company called and said that a helicopter pilot had radioed in that he would come and get him. We were so glad, and then we heard it coming. Roger was trying to talk, and we told him to shut up. Roger heard the chopper also. The pilot was on our frequency and said he'd be right there. He asked if there was a safe place to land, and we told him we had secured a wide enough area for landing.

At that point we spread out in a circle with our flashlights. I told the pilot that when he was directly over us we would turn on our flashlights all at once. The pilot kept asking about the landing zone, and I didn't blame him. We gave him a lot of credit for even trying. We told him that he was almost overhead and our wounded was ready for pickup. The pilot told us to put the flashlights on, and we did. We all held our flashlights straight up into the sky, and then that chopper came down. All I could see was a little green light next to the helicopter door. There were no other lights on that aircraft, and all we wanted was for that helicopter to swoop in and grab Roger and swoop out. Sure enough, in less than a minute, Roger was gone, and as the helicopter pulled away we started yelling thanks to that pilot and the crew.

I never heard what happened to Roger. His name is not on the Wall, and I'm glad for that. As for that helicopter crew, well, let's just say they earned our highest respect that night. After the chopper took off, we waited for Charlie to return. We wanted them to return, but they didn't.

Sunrise came and we picked up Roger's gear and headed back to base. We went back to our hooch and put Roger's gear on his cot, and nobody said a word. So many times we would come back to the hooch after someone was gone, and we would never touch anything on his cot. Eventually someone would pick it all up, but never while we were there.

The captain sent for me, and I was told to report right away. So I went to headquarters. I went inside and they told me to go right in. The captain said we did a good job getting Roger out. He then asked me how I felt about taking over as squad leader. He said because I had been a radio man since day one, I had the knowledge of the duties of a squad leader. I told him that I was eighteen years old, and some of the guys in the squad were in their twenties. He said to me, "You're all marines," and then he shook my hand.

REST AND RELAXATION

So after carrying that radio for almost eight months, I was about to go on patrol without it on my back. And patrol we did—nothing ever changed there. I was promoted to corporal. We always stayed off the trails. We always used rice paddies to walk through. We always looked for caches and bunkers; nothing ever changed there either. Anything that looked suspicious was destroyed; any possible booby trap was destroyed; and we didn't play around. *Bang*, it was gone.

Now we would be lining up for patrol with Lee Bollinger (the Bull) at point; Mike Moore (Flaky Jake), the cover man; myself; then Tom Brennan (Tommy) with radio; George Grey (the Weasel); Don Anderson (Andy); Bob Semple; David Kitchen; Pat Barker (the Bear); and Bill Tangway (the Count) at the back door. It was a heck of a time for me to become squad leader because I was going on R&R soon, but we went out and did quite a few patrols before then. I couldn't wait. *Taiwan, here I come*, I thought. *Destination Taipei.*

I said good-bye to the guys and got on the truck and, with papers in my hand, I headed for the airport. I boarded a flight bound for Taipei, and off we went. I had two thousand dollars with me, and I was ready for whatever was about to happen. I sat next to a guy who was in the air force, and he was staying in the same hotel I was, so we decided to team up. So after we landed, we shared a cab to the hotel, and it was really funny when we got near downtown. We both sat in the back of the cab, and all we could hear were horns blowing. We looked at each other and laughed because the drivers were crazy. Everybody was honking their horns. Everywhere we went they honked. So this was Taipei. We went into the hotel together, and we both checked in. The air force guy was kind of dorky, so he went his way and I went mine.

As soon as I checked into my room, I picked up the phone and tried to call my parents. The operator told me that it would take some time and that they would call back when my parents were on the line. I said OK and hung up. I couldn't wait to go out on the town, and my money was burning a hole in my pocket, so I went downstairs and looked around. I noticed the cars in the street were still honking their horns. I saw what looked like a fancy restaurant across the street, so I went over, and the place was packed. There were lots of servicemen and lots of women, so I decided it was time to rest and relax.

It didn't take long for me to meet a young lady who spoke very good English. She was a knockout, with long, shiny black hair. We got a table. I was starving. Thank God the menu was in English. We got our food, and boy did I eat everything on my plate. She asked me if I would like a tour of the island, and I said sure. My vacation was now in full swing. Then we left the restaurant, and she said she wanted to show me around the city. I agreed. I told her I would like to see everything. Taipei was beautiful except for the horns. They never seemed to stop, and neither did the drinks. I got drunk that night. Boy, did I get smashed.

After a day of sightseeing and drinking, it was time to go back to the hotel. I asked at the desk if any phone calls came for my room or any messages. They said no, so I went up to my room and fell asleep. It was about four in the morning when my phone rang, and the operator said that she had a person-to-person telephone call for Jim Jordan. It was my mom. That was my first communication by phone to my mom in nine months; needless to say, it was great to hear her voice. Then I talked to my father, my uncle, and my brothers. I was on the phone for over an hour. They kept asking me about everything, and they were all concerned about Golf Company. Later on I found out that that phone call cost my parents five hundred dollars.

The next day my tour guide and I drove out into the country to see all the sights that could be seen. I remember a gigantic clock made out of flowers with the ocean as a backdrop. It was gorgeous. Believe it or not, sometimes I felt funny without my weapons. We did everything together, and she stayed with me for my entire vacation. Near the end she asked me if I would like to meet her family, and I said sure. We drove about two hours outside the city to a small village that looked a lot like 'Nam. I started to feel funny. I thought they knew who I was and what I did in 'Nam. I knew it was crazy, but I started to think I was being set up, and I thought the cabdriver was in on it.

She took me into a house and introduced me to her father and mother and then took me into a room and showed me her baby. My imagination had run away with me, and I felt embarrassed. Anyhow, we stayed there maybe an hour. Then we got back in the cab and headed back to the city. My stay in Taiwan was all but over for me the next day. I'd be back in 'Nam, but I'd had a wonderful week. I ate a lot and I drank a lot. I saw everything there was to see on the island.

The next morning I packed my stuff and got ready to call for a cab to the airport. I told her that she had been great company for me. I reached into my pocket and counted my money. I had about six hundred dollars left. I kept twenty dollars and gave her the rest. It's funny, but when I was leaving that island, I thought I would never survive Vietnam.

A GRUNT'S RITE

Well, my vacation was over, and it was time to go back to the base. I brought back some snacks for everybody, and they told me that while I was gone we'd lost one of our squad members, David Kitchen. David was a very quiet kind of guy. He was soft-spoken and real thin, and he never complained about anything; he was liked by all of us. His death hit us all a little harder than those of all the other guys because he was a guy from Kansas who was like a kid brother to us all. He had a childlike smile that made him stand out. I don't think I ever served with anybody else I can say that about. He was like a priest. I had a bag of his favorite pretzels that I'd brought back for him in my hand, and as I looked at them I asked those guys how he got it. Weasel spoke up and said he and David were paired up together in an ambush and a sniper took him out. I'll never forget George's face when he said, "He was right next to me; it could have been me."

We kept up our patrols and ambushes day and night, always rotating with our platoons. The VC were also out there day and night. We never gave up, and they never gave up. They were sneaky, and we were sneaky. They had one advantage, though, and that was the people in the villages. I don't know why, and I never did understand why, but they would hide and protect the enemy. It seemed funny to us that we were defending people who were defending the enemy. I don't care what anybody says: They did protect them, and we knew it. We knew that it fell on deaf ears when we brought it up, so we gave up talking about it and just did our jobs the best we could every day.

If there was one thing that I learned, and we all learned, it was that we had a "grunt's rite." That rite was that if you were wounded or harmed in any way, you would be protected at all costs, and that was our number one commitment. All we had was each other, and we knew it. If we were in pursuit of the enemy and someone was wounded, we would immediately stop our pursuit and care for our fallen brother. Our grunt's rite would automatically kick into action. We would surround that soldier and tend to his wounds. If there wasn't a corpsman with us, we would do the very best we could bandaging him up. We were pretty good at that. At the same time we would call a medevac and look for a spot for the helicopter to land.

We were aware that the VC and the NVA knew that if we stopped our pursuit it was probably because one of us was wounded, and they knew that a helicopter would soon be landing. So a lot of times they would circle back and position themselves for the arrival of the helicopter. We didn't care about Charlie; our number one priority was the evacuation of our wounded. From time to time we would hear that the enemy had obtained American radios and that they would listen in on our conversations. There was nothing we could do about that, so we knew that there was a possibility that the enemy could listen in on our conversation with the helicopter pilot. With that in mind, we would be very careful in everything we said.

It was customary that when a helicopter was coming in for a medevac the pilot would ask us to be prepared to throw a smoke grenade to show him exactly where our position was because it wasn't easy finding us in the thick, high weeds. We had heard stories that sometimes a pilot would tell us to throw a yellow smoke grenade so he would know where we were, but at the same time the enemy would also throw a yellow smoke grenade. If the pilot landed at the wrong site, it would be disastrous. So with that in mind, we would wait till the very last second and pop a smoke grenade of a certain color and ask the pilot what color he was looking at. That was the best way to assure the pilot of our exact location.

We would be in a perimeter, and as we waited for pickup, Flaky Jake would walk around the inside of our perimeter with his M79 grenade launcher, looking for anything suspicious. Let me say that Flaky Jake could hit an apple off a tree. If everything went well, we would load our guy or guys on the chopper, and it would take off just as fast as possible. Then we would wait to see if anybody would open up on that chopper, and if not then we would go back on patrol.

If there was one thing the Marine Corps was bad at, it was letting us know what happened to those guys we put on those choppers. We never heard how they were doing or if they made it. Sometimes if a guy wasn't hit that bad, he would come back, and we loved to see them. They would go on and on about how good the food was and brag about their new boots and uniforms, and we would ask them if they saw any of the other guys at the hospital—sometimes yes, sometimes no.

We kept up our patrols, and now we were going farther out, and the heat was extremely hot, and there was never a breeze. During the monsoon season, the rice paddies would fill up very fast, and that would make the rats evacuate their homes. They would head for the hills, some of them the size of cats. I will always remember that monsoon season because the rain just never let up. We were nearing the end of May.

When we got back from patrol, I was ordered to report to headquarters. I didn't know why I was summoned, but I went right away to see the captain. He told me to come into his office and have a seat. Then he held up some papers and read them. He looked at me and said, "Do you know your squad has gone three weeks without a casualty?" I said, "No, sir." He put those papers on his desk and told me that I was doing a good job and to keep up the good work. He then told me to go and get something to eat.

You know, it's funny, but to this day I can never think of anything ever said to me that equaled what he said to me that day. As I walked away, I felt like the proudest guy in the world. I knew it was because of Lee Bollinger, a.k.a. the Bull, our point man; Mike Moore, a.k.a. Flaky Jake, our cover man; Tom Brennan, our radio man; Pat Barker, a.k.a. the Bear; George Gray, a.k.a. the Weasel; Bob Semple; Ray Otto, a.k.a. the Cop; Bill Tangway, the backdoor man, a.k.a. the Count; and my good friend, Don Anderson, a.k.a. Andy; they were the reason. Things were different now that I was a squad leader; now I was making decisions instead of relaying them. Now there was no room for error; now I had to be responsible for a squad of guys and not just myself; now was the time to emulate all the other guys who had stood in my boots before.

On June 2, 1969, our squad was on patrol when we ran into a group of NVA soldiers and they tried to ambush us. The difference between the VC and the NVA was that the VC in civilian clothes would attack us and run away, but the NVA in uniform would attack and stand toe-to-toe with us. Well, we were going toe-to-toe with these guys. You talk about a firefight—this was a firefight. We were very close to each other, shooting clip after clip of ammo.

Then we noticed these two women soldiers that were manning a mortar gun, firing that thing at a rapid pace. They were positioned behind an old tree trunk. I could see their hair flying up and down as they kept loading and loading, and they were getting closer and closer to us, so we knew we had to stop them. They had their mortar hidden, and it was hard to get a good shot at them. They must have set some record that day, shooting off so many rounds in a short amount of time. What amazed me was that one of them looked right at us after every round, and she was yelling to the other one to adjust. They were in a spot, but we could not get a clear shot at them. Even Flaky Jake had a hard time. Because of the trees he could not use his blooper, so they were daring us to do something, so we did.

All the other NVA soldiers were hidden, so we went right for the mortar gun, and there were bullets flying everywhere, but they kept loading and firing, and their hair was still flying. So I split up the squad into two groups: half of us guys would go right for those women, and Flaky and the others would focus on the other group in the bush. We gave them everything we had. We noticed a couple of the NVA soldiers come running over, trying to protect the mortar, but we were focused on stopping that mortar gun. I saw our bullets were right on them and told everybody to keep it up—to watch out for those other NVA soldiers but keep on that mortar gun.

We had split squads at two different angles, firing like crazy, and Flaky's group was keeping the other group pinned down. I could see that we were hitting those two soldiers, but they just kept firing that mortar with their long hair flying up and down. But they were not adjusting the mortar gun anymore, and the shells were going off behind us. Then they slowed down.

A couple of NVA soldiers positioned themselves right in front of that mortar, and they paid dearly for that. I don't know how many times we hit those two women, but they were obviously in bad shape. One of them was yelling to the other for a round, moving her hands; they were looking at each other, but they never looked up at us. By then we were on top of them, and they tried to reach grenades on their belts, still yelling at each other. Then we took them out. It seemed that the other NVA soldiers had had enough and taken off. We picked up the mortar gun and their weapons and brought them back to base.

A couple of days later, a newspaper reporter from the *Stars and Stripes*, the military news, came looking for me. When he found me, he asked if he could talk to me for a few minutes, and I said sure. We walked out toward the bunker, and he told me that somebody had put me up for an award. I didn't know who or why, but he started asking me about capturing the mortar gun, and I explained what we had done. He was asking how we got it, and he was writing everything down. He kept looking at his paperwork as I answered his questions; he kept telling me that Golf Two Bravo's casualty rate was at an all-time low—why? I told him we were just being careful—very, very careful, and lucky. I also told him we had the best squad members in the Marine Corps. We would always rotate our point men, but we had Mike Moore (Flaky Jake) as our cover man, and he was a ringer with his shotgun, Bernadette, or his M79, Blooper, whichever one he decided to carry that day.

He then asked me if I was aware that I had participated in over two hundred patrols and ambushes and a couple of operations and I was still eighteen years of age. I was surprised to hear that, but I had never kept count, and I was a little embarrassed at that question. We then went back to the hooch, and he shook my hand. He then interviewed a couple of the guys and went back to head-quarters. To my surprise he wrote an article in the *Stars and Stripes* newspaper about what we did on June 2.

FRIENDLY FIRE

Our next assignment was a nighttime ambush. We left the compound about two hours before sundown, said good-bye to the guys in the bunker, and off we went, slow and easy, no hurry. We had to be slow and careful at all times because civilians would walk on trails during daylight, and they were working in the rice paddies, so you just couldn't shoot anyone you saw. Believe me, when the sun started to go down, the civilians would hightail it back to their villages, and they never left their huts at night.

We were right on course toward our designated ambush site, and the sun was starting to set. I checked our coordinates as we walked, making sure we would arrive just as the sun was almost down. Before we knew it, darkness was here, and we still had a short walk to go. There was no moon that night. When there was a full moon, you would never walk through an open field, never, but when there was no moon it was considered safe to go through an open field. As we walked through the field, we heard artillery fire from far away; that sound was normal, and we all knew it was friendly.

Then we saw two phosphorus shells land about five hundred yards in front of us. We knew that when there was going to be an artillery barrage, they always started out with phosphorus shells, which consisted of white smoke. That served as a starting point for the live rounds that we knew would follow. How in God's name could they be firing at the position we were supposed to be nearing? We stopped and looked at one another in shock, and we actually started to talk to each other out loud, which was a no-no, but what the hell were we going to do?

Just then the shells started to fire for effect. They landed about four at a time, and they seemed to be heading slowly in our direction. We started to panic. We had never encountered anything like this before. We knew we couldn't outrun it, so I grabbed the radio and told everybody to dig in. The rounds were dropping fast, and it was getting louder and louder. I called Golf Company. I knew we didn't have a lot of time, and I knew that by the time I told Golf what was going on, they would have to look up where we were, then call artillery, and tell them to stop shooting at those coordinates.

So I did something you are not supposed to do. I told everybody to form a circle around me, and in the middle of the field I dropped down to the ground and pulled out my map. I told the guys to turn on their flashlights and keep their legs together to try and hide the light. As they turned on their lights, I read the coordinates and yelled them out for Golf Company. I kept yelling for a cease fire and saying those coordinates over and over. We quickly turned our lights out and went back to digging just as fast as we could. But the ground was hard as a rock, and our shovels weren't getting it done.

The rounds were heading right for us. Now it was getting louder and louder, and somebody started to pray out loud, and then all of us started to pray out loud. I could hear the shrapnel flying over our heads and hitting the trees and the earth shaking. At that point I was prepared to die. I said an "Our Father," and there was nothing more I could do. I didn't know how close those rounds were to us, and I don't ever want to know, but suddenly they stopped. Right after they stopped, I could still hear the shovels and the prayers, and then we heard nothing.

At that point I was shaking like crazy, and so was everyone else. We couldn't believe what had just happened to us. How could they screw up like that? How could they not know where we were supposed to be? Things could have been much worse in just a few more seconds. We just lay there for a while, and everybody was thanking God and at the same time cursing all around.

Golf Company called to ask about our situation, and we said that we were all alive and that the shelling had stopped and we would be going to our ambush site as soon as we could. As I lay there, I was thinking about how close I had just come to dying, yet I was prepared to die, and it was a peaceful feeling that I had within myself. I think all of us had that same kind of experience that night. We then got up and started to move out to our checkpoint. I turned around and looked at a half a hole I had dug and wondered what if.

We stayed out there that night, finished our ambush, and then headed back to the base. The topic of the day was how in the hell that could have happened. When we returned to base, I went right to headquarters, reported in, and very calmly asked what went wrong, but nobody ever answered me. But all day long, I kept finding packs of Marlboros on my cot and a couple of cans of spaghetti and meatballs.

CHINESE POW

毛澤東

We were going out on a daytime patrol, and this one was going to be all day. We would depart at seven o'clock in the morning, so we lined up and off we went. It was clear skies and ninety degrees, and we were only out about forty-five minutes when we saw a North Vietnamese soldier taking a shit by the side of a trail. He had no weapon, only toilet paper, and we scared the hell out of him. Flaky Jake was holding his blooper, smiling at me, and said, "Say when, JJ." We didn't fire on him, and he pulled up his pants and started running just as fast as he could, and we started running right after him just as fast.

We only made it about thirty yards when we came to an open field, and then we saw a pretty big molehill, and we saw a hatch starting to close just like a submarine hatch would. We now knew where he was, and we circled that molehill and started to laugh. A couple of the guys started to grab hand grenades, and I said no.

Those guys started looking at me like I was crazy and said, "What do you mean, no?" I said that he had no weapon and nobody got hurt, and he was just taking a shit. I shrugged my shoulders and said, "Let's see if we can take him alive," and those guys didn't want to hear that. They wanted to frag him right away, and believe it or not I think it was the first time we ever disagreed on anything. But I was the only guy holding things up, and I just kept saying the guy didn't do anything wrong except get caught. Maybe it was my upbringing, but I thought it was wrong to frag him that day. We were kind of arguing, but I really thought it was the right thing to do at the time. I saw that the guys were pissed off, but I just couldn't do it.

After about two minutes of everybody staring at me, somebody said, "OK, how are we going to get him out?" I said I didn't know, but I really thought it was going to be impossible. But at least the tension between us was over. We started thinking that if we lifted the hatch up there would be some bullets or grenades thrown at us, so what would we do?

All the time we were talking about it, I heard guys saying, "Fuck him," "Frag him," and "Let's get this over with, JJ." Somebody always carried a bag of smoke grenades, so I asked for one, and he handed me a green smoke grenade. I told everyone to be careful, and we all watched that hatch for any movement. I said I was going to throw the smoke grenade in, and if there was retaliation of any kind we would frag him. Besides, we didn't know if there was more than one guy in there.

So everybody was ready, and I lifted the hatch just enough so the grenade could fit in, and then I jumped off the hill and watched as the green smoke started to pour out. We didn't hear anything at all, and we waited, and still nothing. I could still hear somebody saying, "Come on and quit fucking around with this gook and end this thing," but I was determined to try to get this guy alive. I asked for another grenade, and he gave me a red one, and again I tossed it in, and again we waited as the red smoke poured out of the hatch, and again nothing.

Then we started to think maybe there was a back door or something like that, and we started looking around, but we couldn't find anything. So I asked for another grenade, a different flavor, and this time it was yellow. Again I tossed it in, and guess what— we heard movement, and that guy was coughing and gagging like crazy. It sounded like just one guy was in there, and then we saw the hatch get thrown open, and the smoke was pouring out. We had our weapons at the ready and were staring at that hatch, not knowing what to expect. At this point anything could happen

We could hear him gagging and coughing, and we saw his hands sticking straight up, and we were all yelling, "Watch out, watch out, watch his hands." Then we saw his arms, and he was gagging like crazy as he started to emerge from that tunnel. Everybody was yelling, "Watch him and look for a trap or something." He reached the top of the steps and rolled out and down the molehill and was on his hands and knees, just coughing and gagging and spitting up. We immediately frisked him, and he had no weapons on him, no wallet, and no hat. He was busy gagging and trying to breathe as we went through his pockets. I pulled out a flag that was in one pocket, and from the other pocket I pulled out at least fifty condoms. We all laughed when we saw them; that was all he had on him.

But as we looked at him, we noticed something strange about him. He looked like a tie-dyed doll; he was covered from head to toe in green, red, and yellow. We saw his uniform, and it was Chinese. *Oh my God, we caught a Chinese soldier.* When we stood him up, we saw how tall he was, and I looked at the flag he was carrying, and it was a flag with Mao Tse-tung on it. He looked like an officer, but we weren't sure.

We then tossed two regular grenades into that bunker. I told Tom the radio guy to call Golf Company and tell them we captured a Chinese soldier and that we would be bringing him back.

Golf Company called back and said, "What did you say?" We said again that we captured a Chinese soldier and were bringing him back. They laughed and said, "Roger, Golf Two Bravo."

All that guy did was cough and spit, and I felt a little sorry for him. Then we started to laugh at the way he looked—he looked like a clown. When I tried talking to him, I could see the inside of his mouth, and it was loaded with smoke. I'll bet he didn't stop coughing for thirty minutes. In the meantime Golf Company called back to verify that we did indeed capture a Chinese soldier, and we said, "Absolutely we did; yes, we did." They then said that someone from intelligence would be waiting for us when we got back, and we said, "Roger, over and out." Tommy, the radio operator, said he was getting calls from different squads asking if it was true, and he was laughing, saying, "Yes, we did."

As you have figured out by now, we never saw or heard of Chinese soldiers where we operated, and we felt like we had something very rare and couldn't wait to get back to base. Golf Company called again, telling us to hustle it up, and I heard Tommy telling them we were moving as fast as we could. Now we were in eyesight of the compound, and we could see about twenty guys standing next to the Golf bunker. Then there were forty, and then there were sixty.

As we were zigzagging through the wire, we all turned around at each other, laughing. Then there must have been one hundred guys, and they started yelling and clapping, and we felt like celebrities. I saw a couple of officers whom I didn't recognize, and they walked up to me and said, "What the fuck did you do to that guy?" I explained how we got him, and I gave them the condoms, but I kept the flag. I knew they would never let me have it, so I never told them about it. They then asked me where on the map exactly we had captured him. They took him away, and we never heard of him again. As we walked back to our hooch, guys were high-fiving us. It was something different, anyhow. And it cut our patrol in half.

As soon as we got in the hooch, I pulled out the flag and had everybody sign it. I still have that flag, and after thirty years I put it in a frame. It reminds me that there is some guy walking around in China who's lucky to be alive.

BIRTHDAY

It was June 25, my birthday, and the guys had a little sing-along. We were all like brothers, and there wasn't a day that went by without us watching each other's backs. We laughed together, and we cried together; we ate together; we slept together; we patrolled together; we fought together; we did everything together all day long, every day. How could anybody be closer?

It was painful, to say the least, when one of us was wounded or killed. No words could describe our feelings when we were waiting for a chopper and heard the engine far away, knowing it was coming as we held our wounded, patching him up and telling him not to worry, everything was going to be all right, as bullets were flying by our heads; then hearing it closer and louder, and as the chopper landed it was so loud you couldn't hear anything. Then we would put him on that helicopter and watch it pull away. We would stare at that chopper pulling away until we couldn't see or hear it anymore, and then we would look at one another with pain and sorrow. We would hold back the emotion that we all felt and somehow continue on our mission with his blood all over us.

It happened so often that after a while it became unbearable, and then you started to think, *When will it be me?* We all got used to that feeling. We all did what we had to do. Yes, we were profession-al soldiers, but I don't think any of us would or could forget what we saw and what we heard or what we felt. I learned a lot in the eighteenth year of my life. I knew then and I know now what Golf Two Bravo meant to me, and I carry that around with me every day of my life. I'm sure all the other guys in all the other squads, platoons, companies, battalions, and divisions felt the same way toward each other, guys from all over America united together, fighting for America, and fighting for each other.

That day was my birthday, and I was now nineteen, and I want-ed to make it to twenty. I knew as long as I was with these guys I had a good chance of making it. Yes, they sang "Happy Birthday" to me, and then they said they were sorry they didn't have any-thing to give me. But they did; oh, yes, they did, and it was so pre-cious. And as I looked at them cleaning their weapons and writing letters, I realized it was the best gift anybody had ever given me.

A PURPLE DAY

On June 30, 1969, we went out on a daytime patrol. The sun was up, and the heat was up too. We were out for about two hours. We got to checkpoint one, and I checked my map. We were right on course, heading for checkpoint two. There were eight of us: no Flaky Jake, no Bull and no Count and no Weasel. We had a new guy at point, and we called him Ring. He was a big guy who was learning the point, and he was good at it, but I was worried about his height because he was at least six foot five, and that was a little high for point. But that was what he wanted to be, and he did real good. We had three guys from the M60 gun crew along with us because we were short on guys, and they'd said they would go along to fill in the squad.

Then we got hit hard. I don't know what happened, but I woke up covered in blood and dazed. I looked around and saw five of the eight of us down. That day I looked at Tommy, our radio guy, and he was out cold, lying on his stomach. I saw Ring, our point man, out cold, and the back of his head was in bad shape, and two other guys, both out cold. I had been hit with shrapnel in my left hand, my right arm, and a lot in my right leg. I can honestly tell you that I was in no pain. I don't know why, but I wasn't. I could see the three guys from guns running around, checking on the wounded and making sure we were protected. What a mess it was.

I was alert and I knew what to do, but I couldn't move, and those three guys were going from one guy to the next with bandages. I was proud of them. I lay there thinking that our casualty count had just gone through the roof and wondering what the hell happened. I thought we had been hit with mortars, but nobody seemed to know what happened.

I asked one of the guys to get the radio off of Tom's back and bring it over to me. Those guys were yelling at me not to look at my leg, but I knew not to. Tom was still out, and they got the radio for me. I called Golf Company with the bad news and informed them that five of us were down and we needed a medevac. I got my map out and gave them our coordinates, and then I read the names of the guys who had been hit, like so many times before, but this time I was calling in my own name, and when I gave them the initials and service numbers of the wounded, the operator asked, "Isn't that you, JJ?" I said yes.

Golf Company called right back and told me a chopper was on its way, but we had a problem because there were too many trees where we were. There was no place for the chopper to land, so we had to get out of there and fast. I couldn't walk, and Tom and Ring were still out. We were really worried about Ring's wounds because his head was split open in the back. We were running out of bandages and worried about being attacked. I could handle a rifle, but I couldn't move my legs. Golf Company kept calling back, asking if we all right and if we were under attack. I think the operator was trying to keep me alert because I'd never heard him talk so much. At the same time, we knew we had to move, and we had to move now.

I couldn't help those three guys, and I felt useless, but I could operate the radio, and that was just one little thing those guys didn't have to do. Two of the guys carried me and the radio, and we headed for some type of clearing. Thank God we found one about a hundred yards away. They propped me up against a rock and put the radio next to me and laid a rifle in my hands. I looked up at those guys, and they were sweating like crazy, and they looked worried. I felt so very sorry for them. I lay there watching them run as fast as they could back to get the next guy, and I was powerless to help, but I got on that radio and told them I hoped the chopper didn't get there too soon because we needed time to get those guys out.

It wasn't long before I saw them carrying Ring, who looked in bad shape. As they laid him next to me, I saw those guys were breathing hard and their faces were red. I looked down at Ring, and I had one more bandage and tried to help with Ring's head wound. Then I saw they were carrying Tommy; he was awake but pretty much out of it. He didn't know where he was. I noticed those three guys were switching; one guy stayed guard, and the other two guys carried us out one by one.

Then I got a call from the chopper that he was en route, and he told us to hang in there. I always loved those chopper pilots because you could hear how concerned they were. I could hear it in their voices all the time. By that time we all had lost a lot of blood, and we were all concerned with Ring; he never moved the whole time. I lay there watching those guys running back to get the fourth guy, and I was just so proud of them. Our grunt's rite was being displayed before my very eyes again.

I could hear the chopper coming, and we had one more guy to get. Golf Company wouldn't let up. "What is your status, Golf Two Bravo? What is your status?" I think they were worried that we would be overrun, but I was in a good position to see anybody coming, and I told them we were OK and I could hear the chopper, over and out.

The pilot called and asked me to get a smoke grenade ready and stand by. I asked him to slow it up because we had one more guy coming, and he said, "That's a roger." Then we were all together huddled around that rock, and I began to feel very weak, and I had trouble hanging on to the phone. The three guys who had pulled us out made a circle around us, and they were completely out of gas and were on one knee protecting us. It was quite a sight to see.

The chopper was right overhead, and we popped a grenade. Down they came, and one by one we were put on that chopper, and away we went. I had a chance to say thanks to those three guys on the chopper, and before I knew it we were approaching the hospital. I could hear the pilot yelling that he was going as fast as he could. He was yelling, "Hang on; I'll get you there." Then down we went, and they put me right on a stretcher.

The next thing I knew, they were cutting off my boots and clothing, and I remember a nurse calling over a priest. As they looked at me, I heard the nurse say how young I looked and that I had lost a lot of blood. Then the priest gave me last rites, and I remember thinking, *I must be pretty screwed up for him to do that.* Right after that I was wheeled into a room, and they sat me up and put a needle in my spine.

Then I don't remember anything until I woke up the next day. I was in a bed, and I couldn't move, and I was freezing. Then I saw a guy in a wheelchair and asked him to throw a blanket on me, please. He said I already had five on me and that it was my blood and not to worry. I lay there looking at the ceiling, and I was informed by a doctor that I was very lucky with my leg; that was good news for me.

For the rest of that day, the guy next to me was screaming. I couldn't look over to my right, but he kept screaming about his knees, and I felt so sorry for him. He just yelled and screamed, begging somebody to do something about his knees. Every three minutes that guy would scream for help as loudly as he could. I lay there wishing someone would help him. His voice was like nothing I had ever heard. I then passed out.

The next day that guy was gone, and I got a new neighbor. I could turn my head, so now I could look around and see what was going on around me. That day a general came into our hut and went from bed to bed, giving out Purple Hearts to all of us. He had a photographer with him, and he put a Purple Heart on my chest and had the photographer take a picture of the general and me. They gave me the picture to keep. I would get another Purple Heart later on, and I always like to say that I got two Purple Hearts, and I did. I mean two; I'm not lying.

Anyhow, I stayed in the hospital for a month, and what a month it was: nurses getting me anything I wanted (within reason); "more ice cream, please"; or "I think I'll have another piece of pie, please"; or "how about could you please fluff up my pillow, thank you very much." Then I went to a wheelchair, and then I graduated to crutches, then a cane, and from there on out it was card game after card game, and the nurses wouldn't fluff my pillow anymore and told me to get my own ice cream. *Hey—what happened?*

I was healing pretty well, and I ran into Tommy and asked him if he'd heard anything about Ring. He said that he heard that they sent him to Japan, and that was the last time I ever heard of him. Wherever he is or whatever he's doing, I wish him well. I know his name is not on the Wall, so I'm real glad of that.

Tommy left the hospital and went back to Golf Two Bravo, and I told him that I was too busy playing cards and eating pie. I also told him that I hadn't tried all the flavors of ice cream, and you know what? He cursed at me. I told him that I was going to bring him up for insubordination, and you know what? He cursed at me again.

I spent a month in the hospital, and they had a real problem with my leg. They had to staple my thigh with a thick metal staple. There was a hole in my leg, and I worried about that. Anyhow, they threw me out of the hospital and told me to return to Golf Company, and I did. The guys were glad to see me, but I was happier to see them. I was showing off my brand-new size ten boots and my brand-new pants, and I felt like a model walking up and down the middle of the hooch. I was clean-shaven, and I was getting a little tired of ice cream, and then they put me on latrine duty. *Hey, who's responsible for that?*

Obviously by now Golf Two Bravo had a new squad leader, and he was a good marine, and I knew it. I was called to headquarters and told that I would be going back to Golf Two Bravo Squad and fit for duty. But I had concerns for my leg because it still had a noticeable hole in it, and I was afraid of Agent Orange floating in the rice paddies. I thought it might do something if it got inside my leg. The corpsman said there was no danger with that stuff, but I thought hard about it, and I really didn't like the idea of dipping my leg in it. But I was overruled, and they told me I was going out the next day.

SHORT-TIMER

We had roll call that morning, and we were told it was daytime patrol for us. We would be leaving at nine o'clock, so I got my brand-new rifle ready. There were a couple of new faces in the squad, and I really wanted to help these guys out the best I could.

When it came time for us to line up, I wondered where they were going to put me. I was placed in the seven slot, and all the guys wished me well. Flaky Jake told me not to worry; he would take real good care of me.

Off we went, zigzagging through the wire, and I know I sounded like a real crybaby, but I didn't want to go into a rice paddy with all that shit in it. But I did what I was ordered to do, and we were off and running.

Then we came to a paddy, and I looked ahead to see how deep it was. It was only about knee-high, but oh my God, my boots had never been wet, but they were about to be christened. And yes, they were. We went from one rice paddy to the next, and then I saw that this one was pretty deep, and I slid into that paddy, trying my best not to get my leg wet, but forget it, down it went, and that was the end of that. I tried to teach the new guys everything I knew every chance I got.

I knew that I was soon to be a short-timer, and I was thankful every time we returned to base. I kept writing home, telling everybody that I'd be home soon, and I believed it. I was determined to get home alive.

I would help the guy in front of me and the guy right behind me, and I would show them how to carry their weapons because it was important that your weapon be held in such a way that it could be maneuvered in any direction in a split second. There was a knack for that. I also told them what to look out for and how to step and where to walk. There was a lot to learn, and I liked to teach, and those guys appreciated it. They learned fast. We finished up our patrol and made it back to base. I would write as many letters as I could because I liked writing the words "I'm coming home soon."

The next morning I walked over to the guard bunker to smoke a cigarette. As I looked at the guard on duty, he pointed to a tall tree, and at the top of that tree was an NVA flag. The guard just smiled, so I went to the hooch and asked the new guys to come with me for a minute. I told them to take a look at the top of that tree, and I said to them, "Do you see who you're fucking with?" I said, "Do you know how much nerve it takes to put that up there?" I told them that they wanted us to know that they were out there and would always be there. Even with our scouts out and our squads always going out and in, they put that up there. I tried to tell those guys that this was the kind of enemy we were dealing with.

We went and told Flaky Jake to get his blooper because we had a job for him. He smiled and said, "What do you want me to take care of?" We all walked over to the sand dune, and then he saw it, waving ever so slightly as he aimed. We had to get an OK before we could fire that weapon because somebody might be out there, and Company said to go ahead. So Jake aimed and said that he wanted to hit that flag with just one shot because number one, he was the best M79 man on the planet, and number two, he wanted to show the NVA if they were watching that he was the best M79 man on the planet.

So he took his time, and sure enough, he hit the branch that the flag was on and stood there shrugging his shoulders. We all started yelling, "Take that, you fucking assholes" and "Up your ass, Charlie!" We were yelling as loudly as we could, raising our arms and giving them the finger, hoping they were watching. Jake just walked back to the hooch, holding up one finger. God, he was good with that blooper.

We then went out on an operation. I think the name of it was Dodge City. It was a perfect opportunity for me to really help the new guys, and I didn't waste any time. I explained everything we did and why we did it. I knew that my time was getting short, and the closer I got to my last patrol, the more the guys would worry about me. Every time we got into a firefight, somebody always seemed to be around me, and I knew why. And when the shooting stopped, I saw all the guys turn around just to check on me.

I was now officially a short-timer, and everyone in the squad and platoon knew it. Golf told me no more patrols for me, and then we were sent to the bridge to guard it. That was where I ended my tour of duty, and I will never forget my last night. We sat around watching the sun go down, and I felt like a priest in a confessional box because one by one the guys came up to me, asking me to do favors for them when I got home, like drink or eat something for them, or just stupid requests. I told them I would, and I told them I would go to Washington, DC, and protest alongside my fellow veterans.

I told them that when I landed in Philadelphia, I wouldn't tell anybody. I said I was going to take a taxi home, then get out and give the driver a twenty-dollar tip, then walk up my street to my home. Everybody listened to every word I said. This was my last night. I didn't want to leave them guys, but life goes on, and I knew that.

After all those patrols and ambushes, all the radio checks and medevacs and operations, it was my turn to go home. I gave away all my little trinkets. The hardest was saying good-bye to the Weasel and Bull and then Flaky Jake. I felt like I was abandoning them. It was hard.

The next day a truck came just for me, and it was time to go. It wasn't easy, but I got on that truck, and as it pulled away I stood in the back and waved. They were yelling and screaming, and I thought I saw a moon. That was a moment in my life that I was so grateful for, to be so happy and so sad at the same time.

We were almost out of sight. I could still see them waving. That was what I had waited for for thirteen months. I looked through the window to see the driver tapping his fingers on the steering wheel. I was going to say something to him, but I couldn't talk. I sat down because I didn't want to get picked off by snipers, and the rest is history.

Just for the record, I did take a cab home. I did give the guy a twenty-dollar tip, and when I walked to my house, it was five o'clock in the morning. I stood there with my duffel bag, knowing I had made it back to where it all started. Home.

One of the neighbors was going to work, and he stopped and shook my hand and said, "Welcome home." That was the first time I'd heard those words. As he walked away, I thanked God for helping me and protecting me. Then I looked at the big sign my parents had on our lawn welcoming me back.

I slowly walked into my house. My uncle was getting ready for work, and he was the first one to see me. He yelled out, and everyone came running downstairs but Mom. My dad said she was kneeling next to her bed upstairs praying. Everybody was shaking my hand and hugging me, yelling and clapping their hands. They were calling people on the phone. Every light in the house was on, but the one person I wanted to see most was Mom, so I had to go up there and get her.

I walked up the steps, but everybody was asking me questions all at once, and the neighbors were walking in the front door wanting to say hello, but all I wanted to do was see Mom. So I said, "Please excuse me; I'll be right down." Then I walked toward Mom's bedroom, and I stood there looking down at her kneeling, with her hands together on the bed, saying prayers out loud and crying.

I stood behind her and said, "Hi, Mom." She stopped praying, blessed herself, and stood up and slowly turned around. Without saying a word, she hugged me so tightly that I still have her finger-nail marks on my back. She held me for the longest time. She still didn't say anything, and then she let go, looked up at me, then turned around and knelt back down. By then my dad was standing in the doorway, telling me to come downstairs because everybody wanted to see me. I didn't want to leave Mom, but I went down to say hello to everybody.

About a month later, I received a registered letter from the Marine Corps asking me to come to the Philadelphia Armory to receive an award. I accepted the invitation, and I was told where and when it would take place. So after one year, six months, and twenty-three days in the Marine Corps, I was discharged, and that was because I had signed up for a two-year tour of duty. But I had one more duty to perform, so I asked my brother Jack, who was still active in the Marine Corps, if he would accompany me for my award presentation. He said yes, so we both put on our uniforms and went to the armory.

I went into a room, and two officers were standing there, and we saluted one another, and they awarded me a Navy Commendation Medal with a combat "V." Then they read my citation and shook my hand; then they tried to get me to re-up, and I said, "Thanks, but no thanks."

I have lived my life since peacefully and with respect, and I never touched another weapon, nor do I want to. I also didn't talk much of Vietnam, and I raised my children to respect our American flag and the history of America, and I would take them to Washington, DC, and we would respect all the memorials to-gether. Now I have a grandson, and I took him to Fort Ticonderoga and explained the Revolutionary War. Then we went to Valley Forge, and I explained what happened there, and we went to the Alamo and Gettysburg, Washington, and to the Vietnam Veterans Memorial at Angel Fire in New Mexico. Most recently we went to Normandy, France, and as we stood on that beach, I explained to him what sacrifices America has endured and why we did and still continue to, to this day.

I'm sixty-two years old now, and I remember that night when we were in the listening post, when we were told a group of NVA was heading toward us, and all four of us said what we would do if we ever survived that night and Vietnam. I said I would never complain, I would marry my girlfriend, live in a small house, have a small family, and hold a career job. And you know what? I rarely complain, I married Marilyn, I've lived in a small house for forty years, we have two children, and I retired from the US Postal Service after thirty-six years.

In 2006 I read that the traveling Vietnam Memorial Wall would be coming to New Jersey, not far from my home. I decided to go and pay my respects. I went to the park where it was erected, and I was by myself, and it was a sunny day, and it was pretty crowded. I knew what panel our guys were on, and I walked along, keeping my thoughts to myself, just remembering all the medevacs and looking at all those names, panel after panel. It started to get my emotions flowing, as it always does.

Then I walked up to these three guys, all dressed in Marine Corps gear with pins and badges, and they were volunteers. I just wanted to be distracted for a moment. I shook their hands and said, "Semper fi." One of those guys asked me what outfit I was with, and I said I was with the First Marine Division. He started to laugh at me, and he said, "Here's another guy claiming to be from the First." I was shocked at what I heard, and I watched all three of them as they kept saying, "Yeah, right; everybody wants to be from the First." They kept high-fiving each other and laughing. I didn't know what to do, and every emotion inside me erupted. I just backed up and kept watching them as they continued to laugh and high-five each other.

I didn't have my discharge papers with me or my Purple Heart or my citation either, and I thought I was going to get sick. I just kept walking backward, not knowing what to do, so I had to get out of there fast. I headed for my truck, just wanting to get away, as far and as fast as I could. As I was exiting the park, I was behind a park ranger who was driving slowly. I wanted to hit my horn, but I thought better of it.

I drove home, and for days I couldn't sleep. It just bothered me to no end, and my wife didn't want to hear it anymore, and neither did my friends and family. So I did a little investigating on the computer and found out that the Second Battalion, First Marines were having a reunion in Houston, Texas, in 2007 and made arrangements to go. My wife and I did attend it, and thank God we did. It was a strange feeling, but I felt like I had to be there in order to get over what those guys had said to me that day at the Wall.

At the reunion we were having a beer and I was telling the guys from 2/1 about that incident, and they couldn't believe what I was saying. But after I told them, it didn't seem to bother me anymore. All of those guys at the reunion did the same thing I did in a far hot jungle called Vietnam. Maybe I don't know all their names or their faces, but I know what they all went through.

I only met two guys from Golf Two Bravo who served with me at the reunion. Their names were Joe Mozzariello, from the Bronx, New York, and Paul Stein, also from New York, who was a corpsman. Joe's health was not very good, and he told me it was because of Agent Orange.

When I went to the 2009 reunion, I was told that Joe had passed away. Joe had been a tunnel rat in Nam, but it was chemicals that got him. I hope to be at this year's 2/1 reunion in San Diego to look for the Weasel, the Bull, and Flaky Jake and to be with my brothers again. I hope to attend every year.
SEMPER FIDELIS J.J. (First Marine Division), over and out.

Made in the USA
Columbia, SC
19 February 2022

56471791R10065